£2.50

CW01604531

# How to DRAW AND SKETCH

Macdonald

# CONTENTS



# HOW TO USE THIS BOOK

Here are step-by-step demonstrations of a range of subjects in different drawing media, designed specially to show you how to draw from a wide range of subjects. To get the most out of these exercises, study each one first and then either re-draw it yourself or, using the same medium, apply the techniques to your own subject.

**Copying.** Don't be concerned about the fact that you are copying these exercises — many famous artists have used other artists' ideas and techniques to develop their own unique style. And copying the exercises will make learning the techniques easier for you as you won't have to worry about finding a subject, composition or design.

**Stay loose.** It is best to attack each subject vigorously, and aim to make a strong drawing. Don't worry about making mistakes along the way — the more you practise and experiment, the quicker and more dramatic will be your improvement in drawing.

**Experiment.** By working boldly and taking risks with lines, colour, shapes and values, you will avoid the risk of your pictures looking tight and overworked. When you are making broad, generous strokes, don't hold your pencil or brush too near the point or your lines will look tentative. Only when working on detail should you hold the pen or pencil close to the point — and keep your details to a minimum when beginning a drawing. Usually they are best left for the finishing touches.

**Keep it simple.** Select simple subjects and compositions to start with. If you are using colour, restrict it to a limited range. Take care not to overwork and smudge the colours, especially if you are using a soft medium such as pastel or charcoal.

If you observe these basic points, you will quickly produce surprisingly good pictures and then you can really start to experiment with bolder compositions, more vibrant or subtle colour schemes, and develop your unique drawing style. *Happy painting*!

A MACDONALD BOOK



First published in Great Britain in 1986
by Macdonald & Co (Publishers) Ltd
London & Sydney

A member of BPCC plc



How to draw and sketch. —
The Macdonald Academy of Art
1. Drawing — Technique I. Title II.
Series 741.2 NC 730

ISBN 0-356-12446-0

This book was designed and produced by
Quintet Publishing Limited
6 Blundell Street, London N7

Typeset in Great Britain by
Facsimile Graphics Limited, Essex
Colour origination in Hong Kong by
Hong Kong Graphic Arts Limited, Hong Kong
Printed in Hong Kong by Leefung-Asco
Printers Limited

Macdonald & Co (Publishers) Ltd
Greater London House
Hampstead Road
London NW1 7QX

# DRAWING MATERIALS

To many the word 'drawing' suggests a work executed in pencil, but a great variety of tools has always been available and the selection is increasing all the time. Today you have a very wide range of materials to choose from. The pencil (from the Latin word pecillus meaning 'little tail') is the most common instrument used for drawing, but coloured pencils, charcoal, pen and ink, rapidograph and felt nibs are all popular alternatives. As you gain expertise and experience, the materials you choose will vary according to your personal style and the nature of the subject.

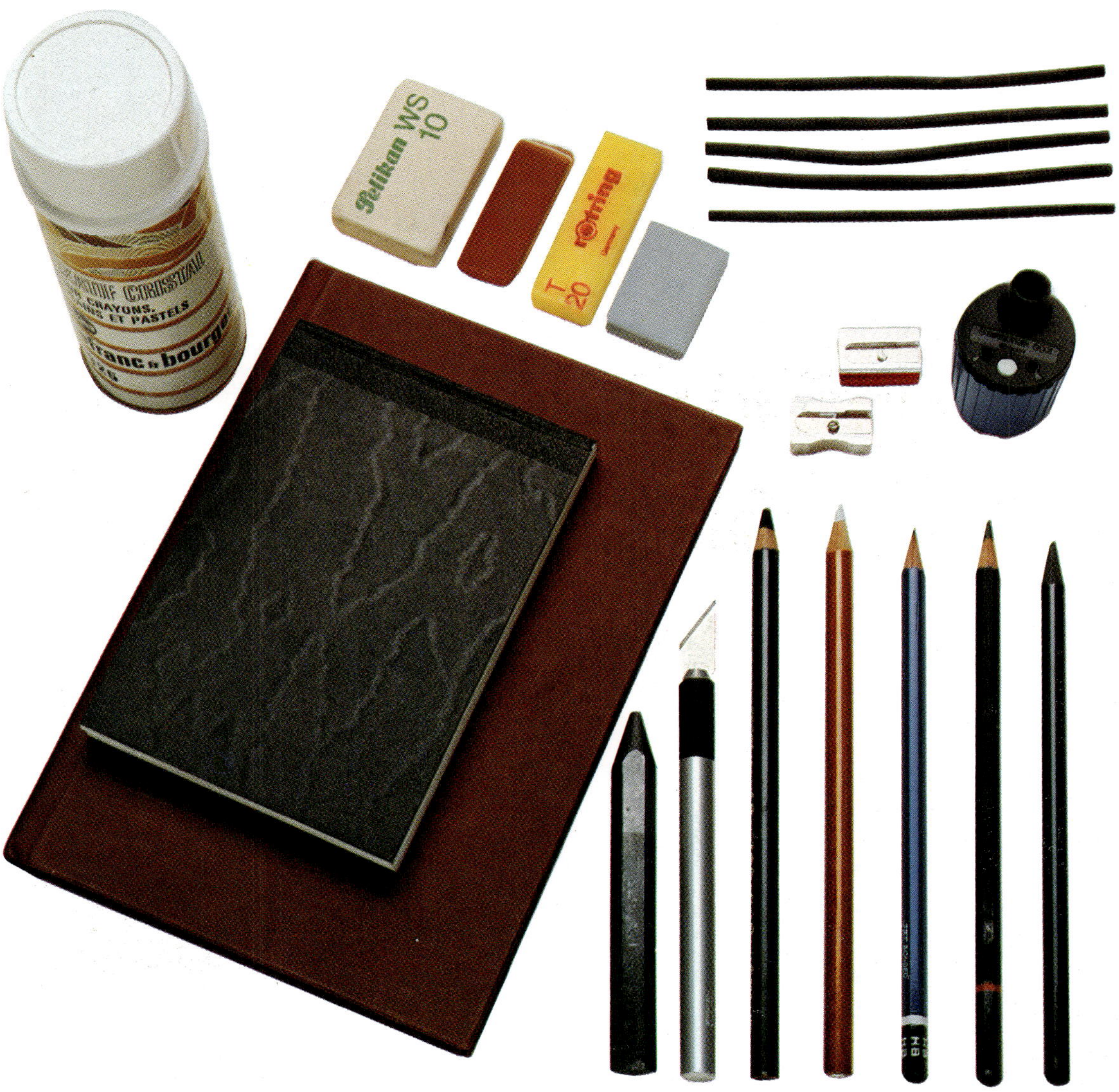

# CHARCOAL AND PENCIL

The traditional pencil is a comparatively new medium in the long history of graphic art, and it was not until 1662 that the first graphite pencil was made. Graphite was discovered in Bavaria in 1400, but its potential for the artist was unexploited until 1504 when pure graphite was found at Borrowdale in England. At first the deposit was thought to be lead and pencils are still sometimes referred to as 'lead' pencils. Until the development of the graphite pencil most sketching and preliminary designs for painting were carried out with a charcoal, or with silverpoint, a silver stylus which required a special ground.

Drawing pencils come in 15 degrees of hardness. The hardest range are the H pencils: 8H is the hardest, H the least hard. F pencils are hard-medium, and HB soft-medium. The softer pencils are the Bs. B is the least soft and 7B the softest. Most artists use pencils that fall somewhere in the range 6H–6B. HB pencils are the most popular pencils for everyday use. Soft pencils have thicker leads than hard pencils, and should be sharpened with a knife or sandpaper rather than a sharpener.

Nowadays refillable pencils are available. The plastic or metal containers hold the lead rods which come in all the degrees of hardness. Replacement leads can be bought separately.

For bolder work, charcoal is still one of the most popular drawing materials. It has a long and distinguished history, and was used by prehistoric cave artists. Charcoal is a carbonized wood made from the peeled twigs of lime and willow trees. The twigs are burned in an oxygen-starved atmosphere until they are completely black and carbonized, but not burnt.

For the artist, charcoal provides a subtle range of tones, including a deep, intense black and it can also be used successfully for drawing in line and tone. It can be a rather messy material to work with and dusts off easily. The best results are achieved on textured paper — charcoal slides over smooth surfaces. All work drawings done in charcoal should be sprayed with fixative to prevent smudging and to preserve the image.

Conté crayons in black, red or sepia are an alternative to charcoal. Made in different grades from medium to extra soft, they lack the crisp freshness of charcoal but they do not dust off and adhere to most types of paper.

*Charcoal* **(below)**. *Compressed charcoal pencils are available in soft, medium and hard grades. Charcoal sticks can be bought in various widths — thick, medium and thin. Powder charcoal is used to produce areas of tone.*

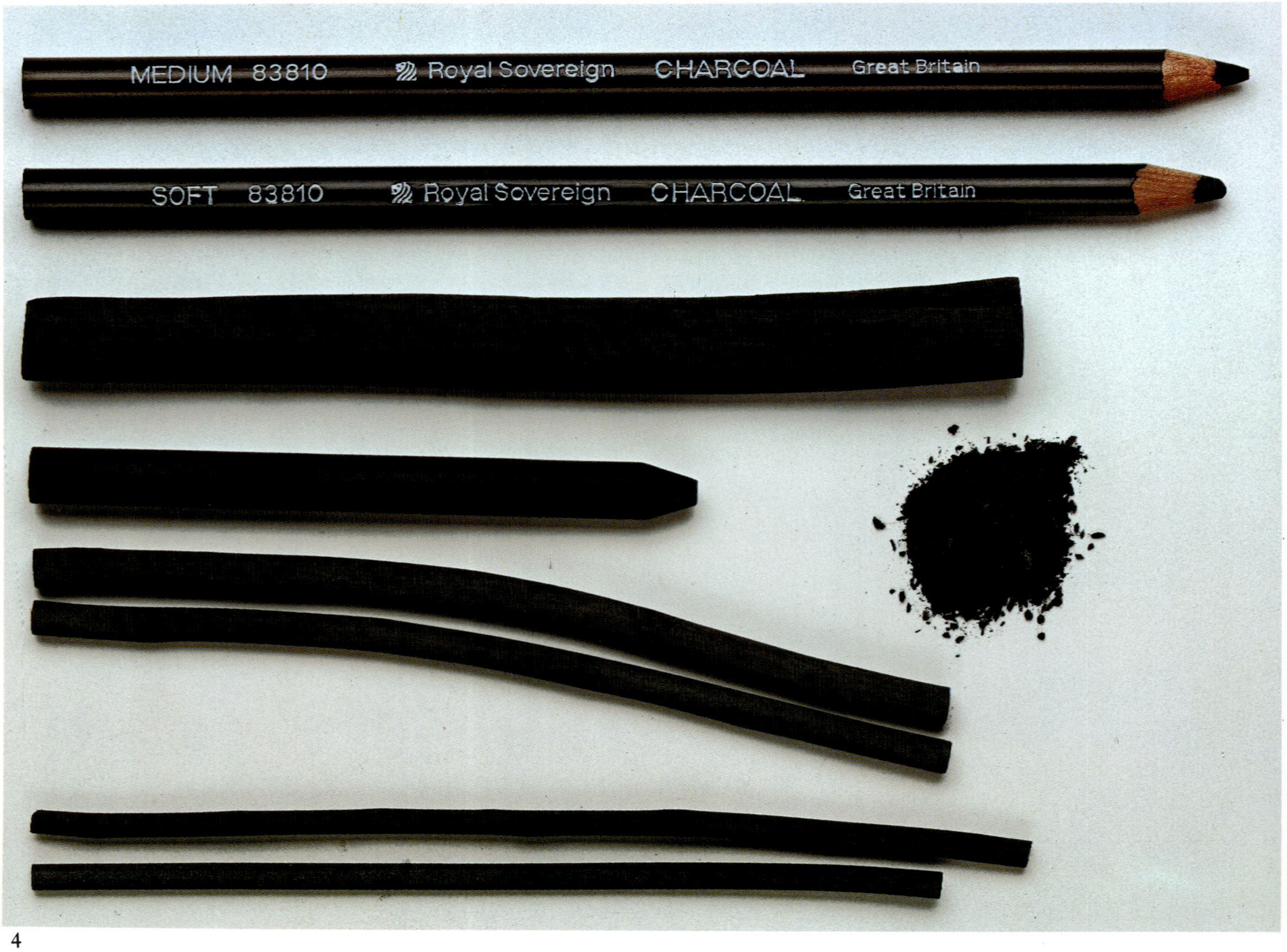

**Pencils (right).** *The range of drawing pencils available to the artist includes the common lead, or graphite, pencils. These range from 7B, the softest, through 6B, 5B, 4B, 3B, 2B, B, H, 2H, 3H, 4H, 5H, 6H, 7H, and 8H, the hardest. Other possibilities are propelling pencils, wax pencils for drawing on acetate, and several series of coloured pencils.*

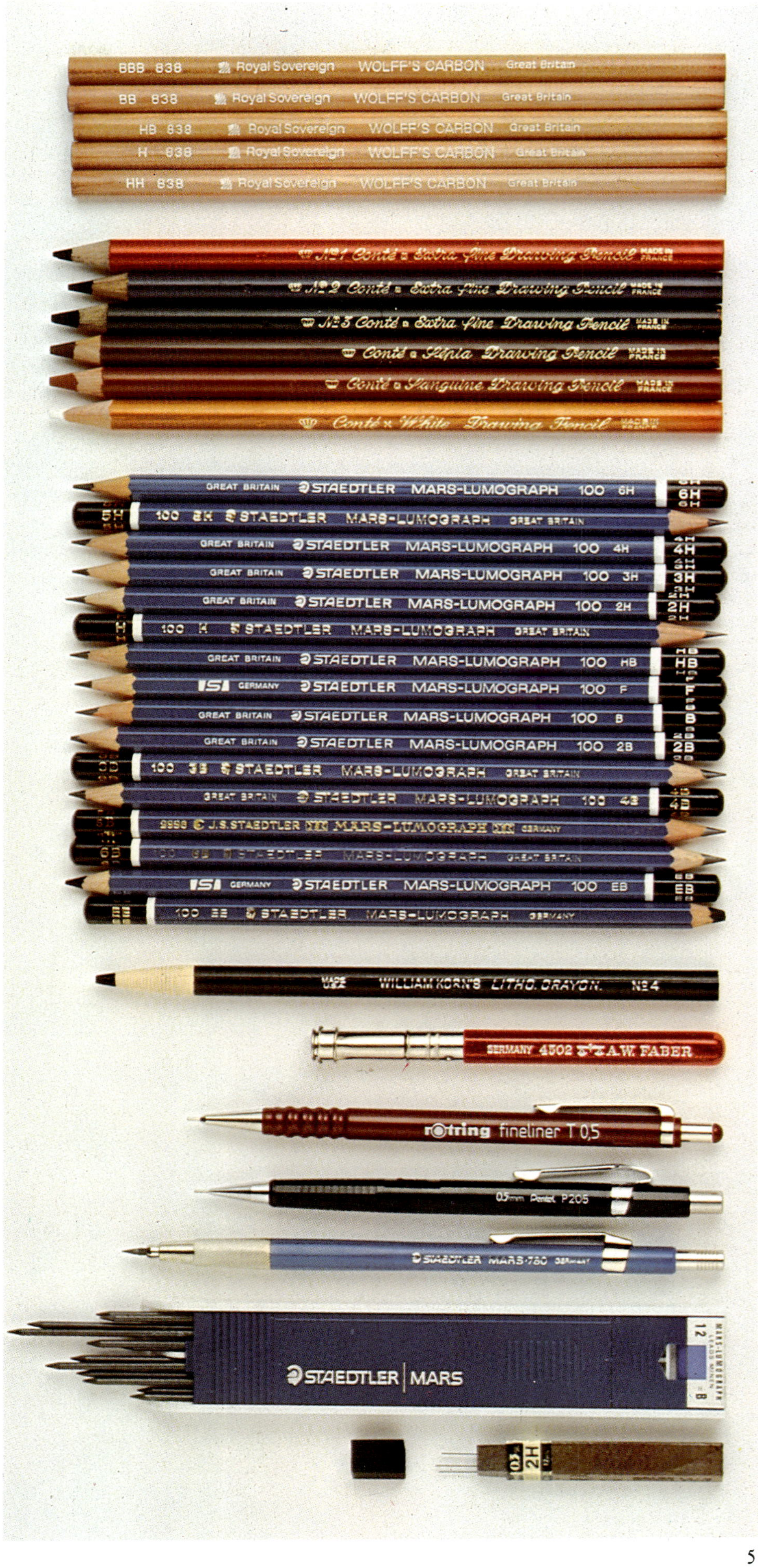

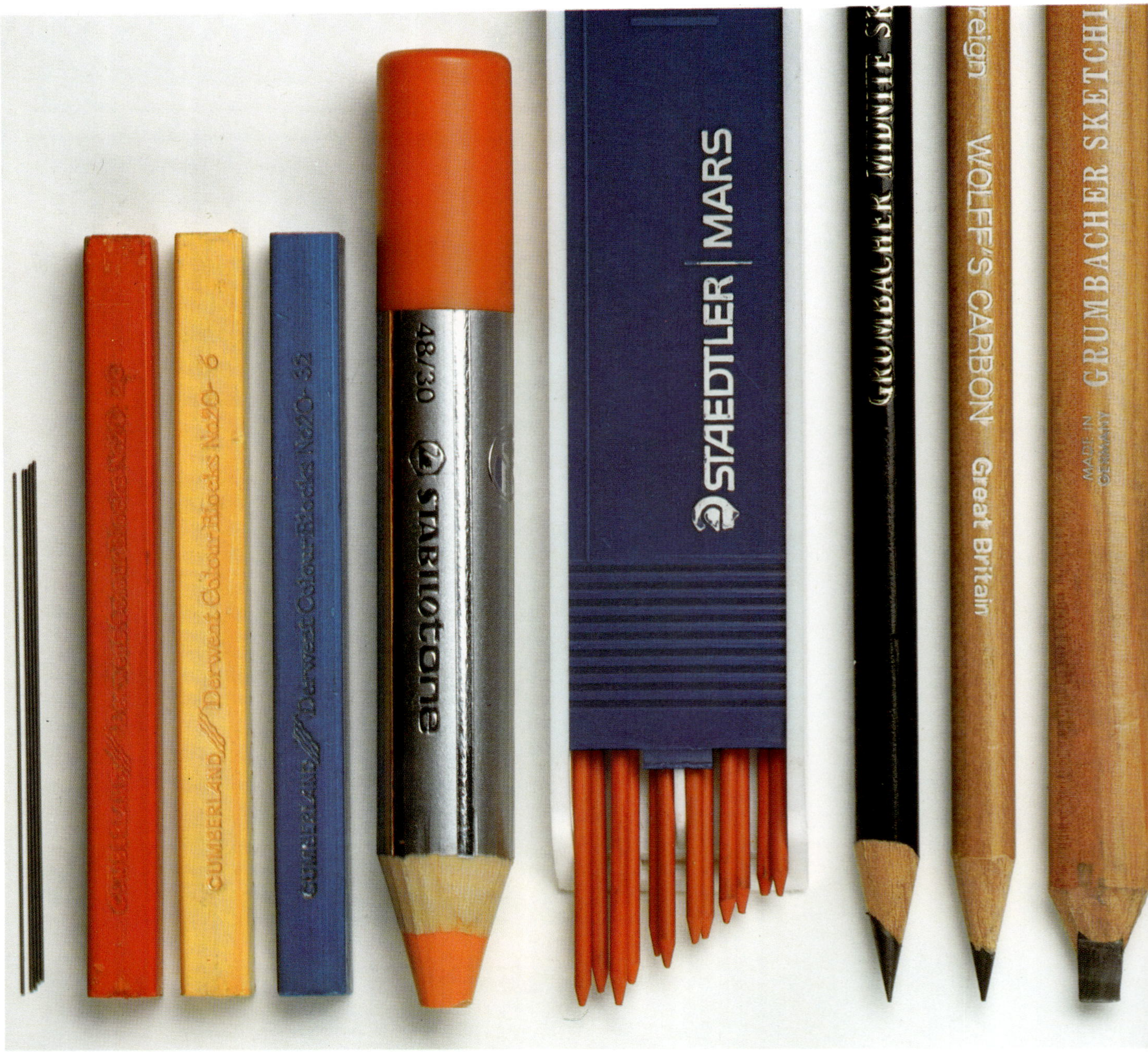


*Coloured Pencils* **(above)**. *The wide range of pencils available to the artist includes* **(from left to right)** *propelling pencil lead, three Derwent colour blocks, Stabilotone wax pencil, clutch pencil leads, Grumbacher midnight sketching pencil, Wolff carbon pencil, Grumbacher flat sketching pencil, 3 Derwent colour pencils, 3 Caran d'Ache Prismal pencils, 3 Carb Othello coloured pencils, All-Stabilo, K and E Audiovisual Projection and Staedtler Mars Omnichrom pencils for film.*

# COLOURED PENCILS

The vast range of coloured pencils now available offers exciting prospects to the modern draughtsman. Not only has the range of colours increased, but manufacturing methods have also been developed to provide products which offer a wide choice of texture and finish. Traditionally, coloured pencils have been popular for making quick sketches and preliminary colour sketches for paintings, but modern artists are increasingly using coloured pencils and felt nib pens in their own right — often to add touches of local colour to an otherwise monochromatic drawing.

Some types of coloured pencil have special properties and can be exploited in different ways. Several brands have leads which are water-soluble, thus allowing you to create areas of flat wash-like colour by simply spreading the pencil marks with clean water. This simple technique

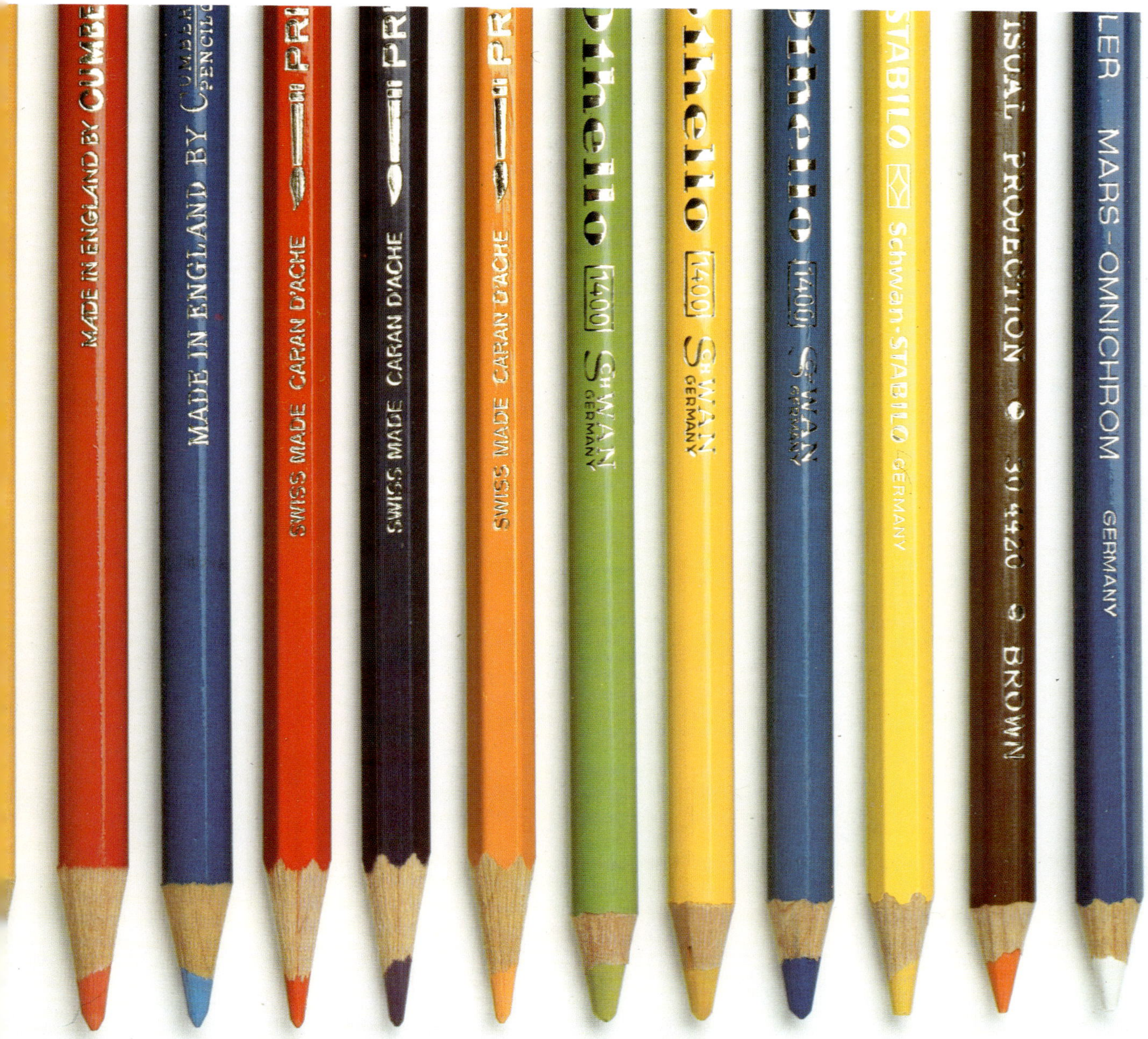


combines the qualities of water colour painting with the delicate, linear effects of coloured pencil. Coloured pencils are easier to control than water colour paint and for this reason may be particularly useful for the artist who prefers to use line but occasionally likes to introduce areas of wash and flat colour effects.

Felt-nib pens — the 'modern' coloured pencils — consist of either water or spirit-based colours soaked into strips of felt or other synthetic material. They are particularly popular in the field of illustration and graphic design where their strong colours and highly contrasting tones make them particularly suitable for print reproduction.

Although some painters feel this very brashness and commercial association makes felt nib pens unsuitable for fine art work, the medium is well worth investigating for its directness and dramatic potential. It is, however, difficult to create subtle colours and finely modulated tonal effects with felt nib pens and the medium should be reserved for bold, colourful effects.

# NUDE IN A SUN HAT

Raw graphite can be bought in powder as well as the more familiar stick form. Used in the powdered state graphite can produce drawings with the soft, grey effects of lead pencil but, in place of the typical linear quality of pencil, you can produce a soft impressionistic effect.

In this drawing the spontaneous qualities of the powder allow the artist to work quickly, describing the basic tones and shapes of the subject, using the fingers to render the contours of the figure with strong directional strokes which both follow and shape the form. It is this particular aspect of the medium, drawing in tone rather than line, which gives graphite powder its unique softness and subtlety. However, pure graphite powder has a slippery quality and because it is so easily applied to the surface the artist must avoid losing control of the drawing. But if mistakes are made they can easily be rubbed out with a rag and turpentine. Because it can be a messy substance to work with, tip a small quantity of powder into a bowl before you start work.

When used with turpentine a range of tones can be created from very pale greys to bold and intense blacks. Coupled with the use of a clean pencil line, the tones of the graphite will lend a soft atmospheric mood regardless of subject matter. Use pencil with the graphite to strengthen the shadows and contours — rubbing harder will darken the tones.

Use a heavyweight cartridge paper or some highly textured support which will allow the powder to grip. Highlighted areas can be achieved by allowing the white of the paper to show through. Alternatively, the graphite can quite easily be rubbed off with a soft eraser.

*Graphite dust is rubbed into the paper with the fingers to give a dense black surface and gradated grey tones. Using graphite dust can be quite messy, so shake a little into a small container before starting work. Start by rubbing a small amount of dust into the paper with your fingers to suggest the darker tones on the subject; mask the drawing with paper to get a straight edge* **(below left)**. *Establish the main shadows with the graphite dust* **(below)**, *before drawing the outlines with a soft pencil* **(bottom).**

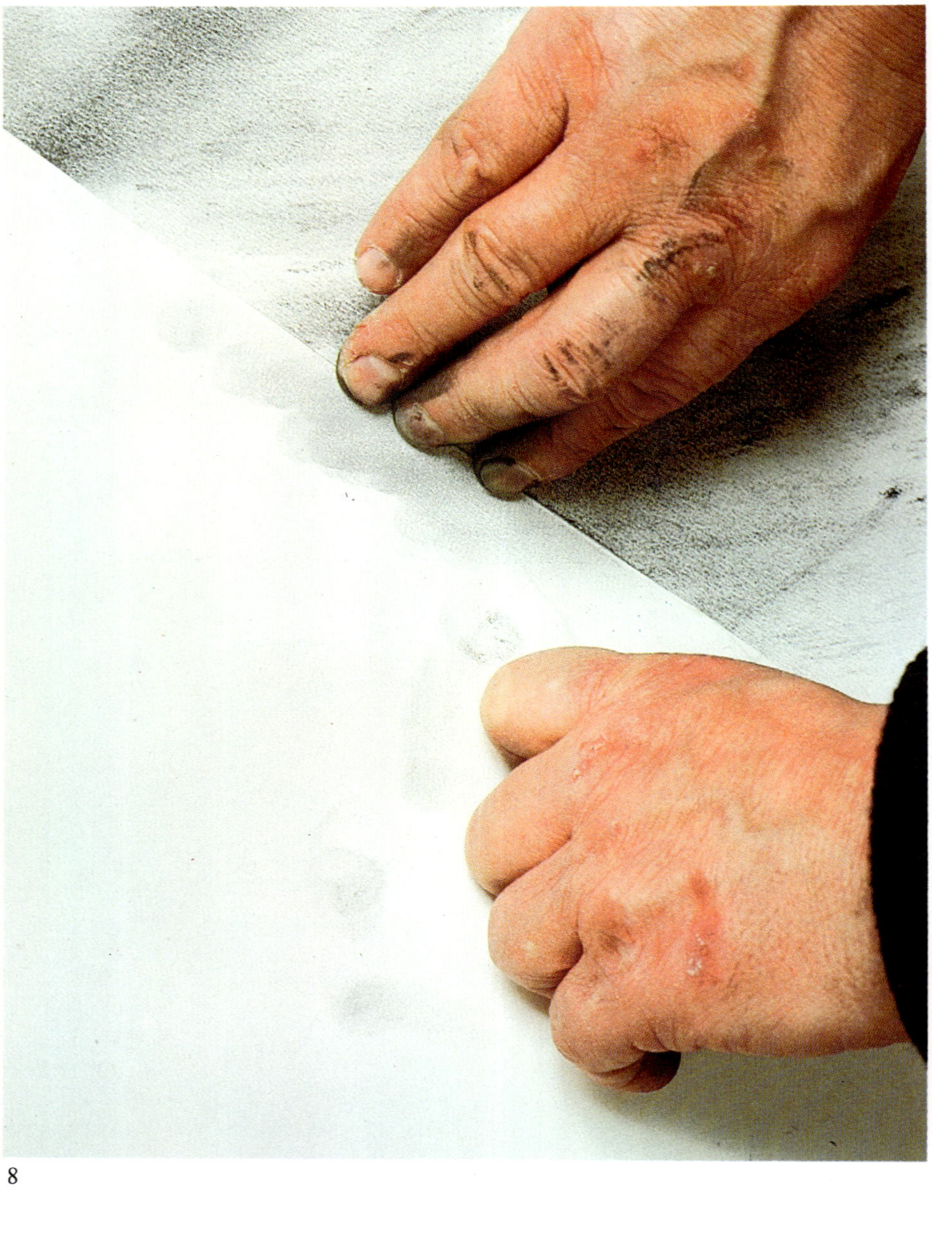

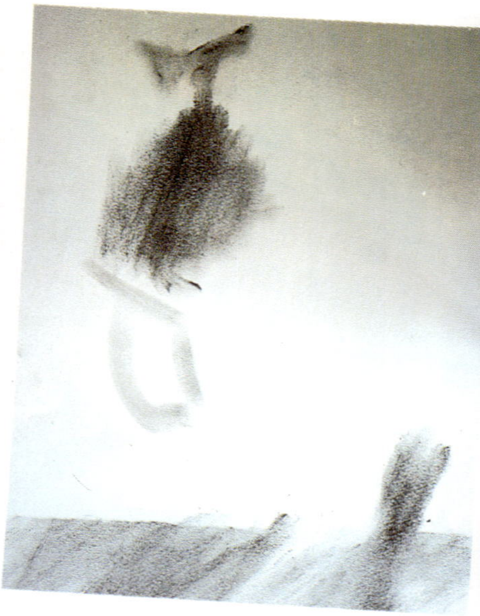

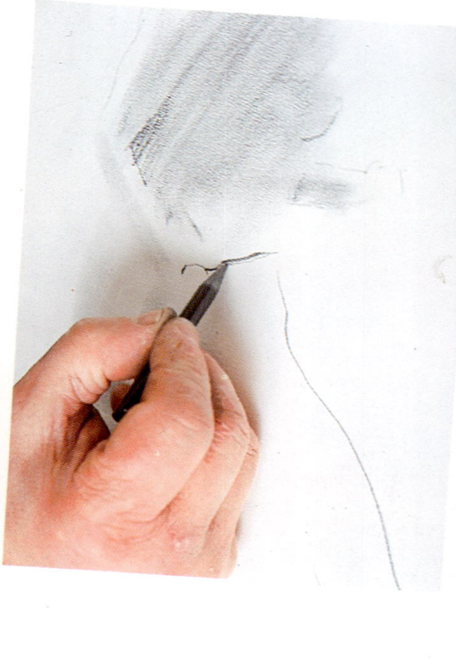

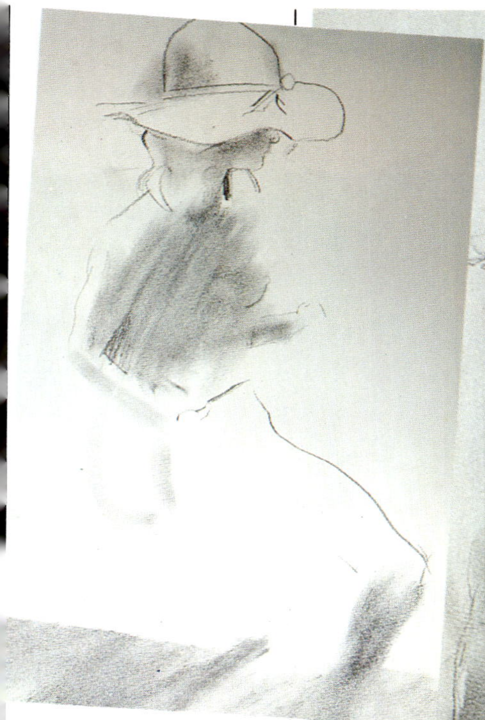

*Use the whiteness of the paper to depict highlights* **(above)**, *erasing the graphite dust with a soft putty rubber where necessary.*

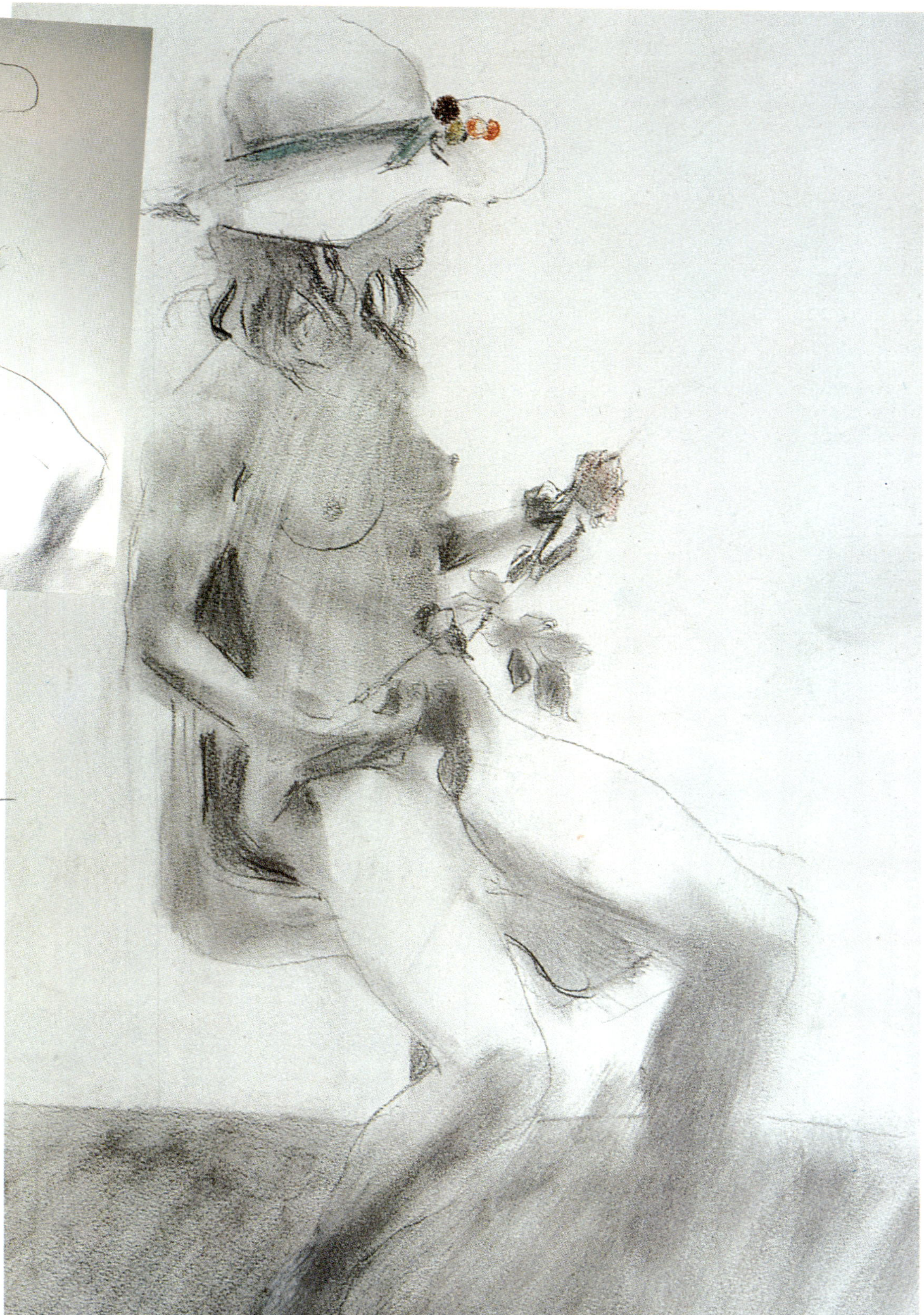

*Develop the drawing by varying the depths of shadow with more graphite and picking out selected details in coloured pencil* **(right)**.

# THISTLE

Pen and ink is especially suitable for tight, detailed work and densely cross-hatched

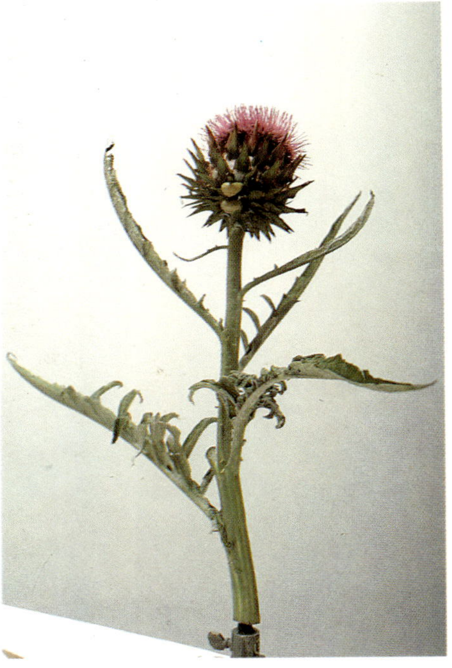

drawing — although it can also be used for loose informal work. When 'mistakes' such as running and smudging are incorporated into the technique a pen and ink drawing can become very exciting.

In this drawing the artist has taken full advantage of the unexpected without losing the strength of the drawing or the character of the subject. Little attempt has been made to control the line of the pen — something many artists struggle to achieve — but, instead, the artist has let the nib catch and jump across the page without interference.

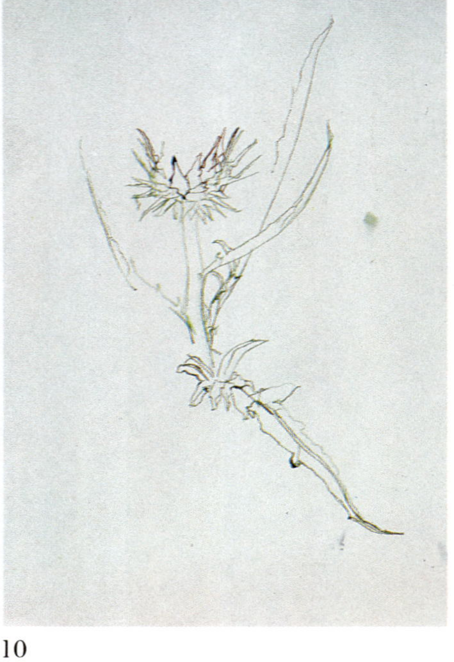

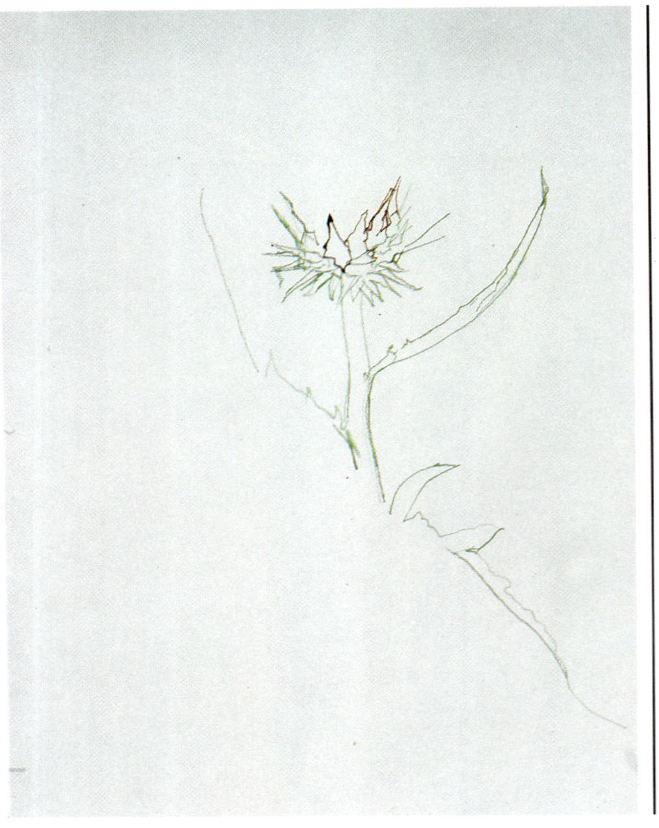

*Use pen and ink to capture the jagged detail and spidery quality of the thistle* **(far left)**. *Dilute the colour by dipping the pen in water and then into green ink. Start to draw the general outline of the subject* **(left)**. *Move down the thistle with green ink, holding the pen lightly to create a rough outline* **(bottom left)**. *Repeat this with red, black and blue ink for the remainder of the outline. Do not attempt to create a tightly controlled drawing, but let the pen drag loosely across the paper. Vary the thickness of the line by turning the pen on its side and pulling it across the surface* **(below)**.

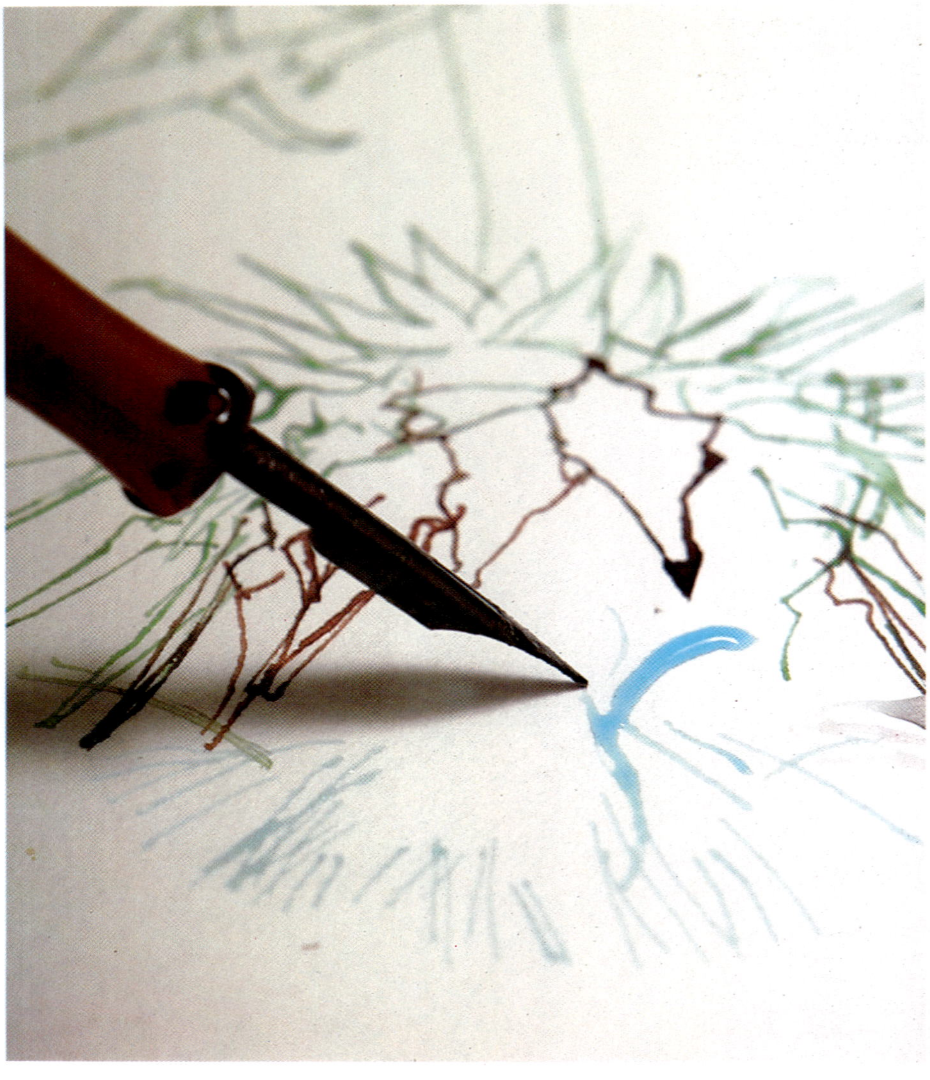

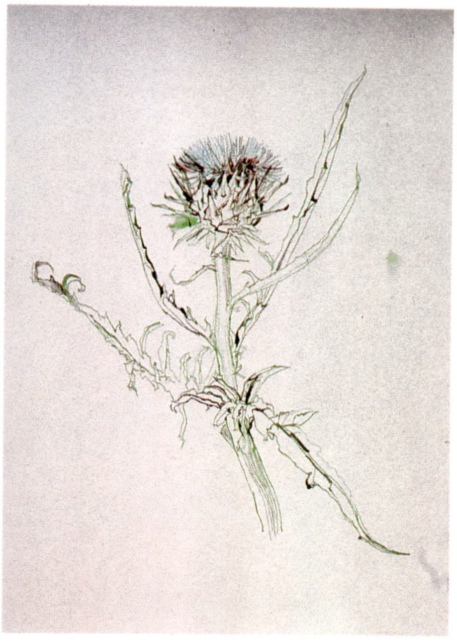

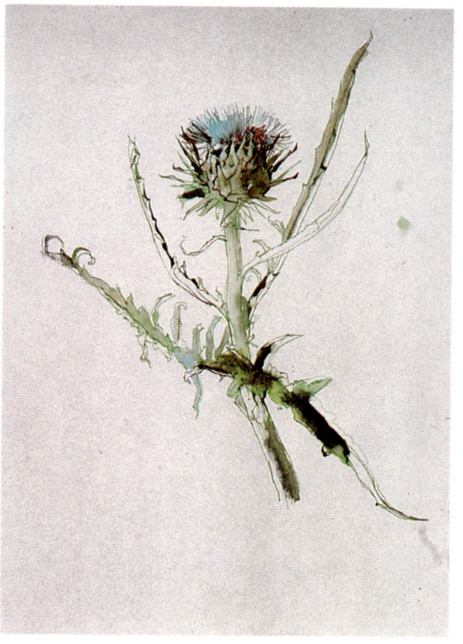

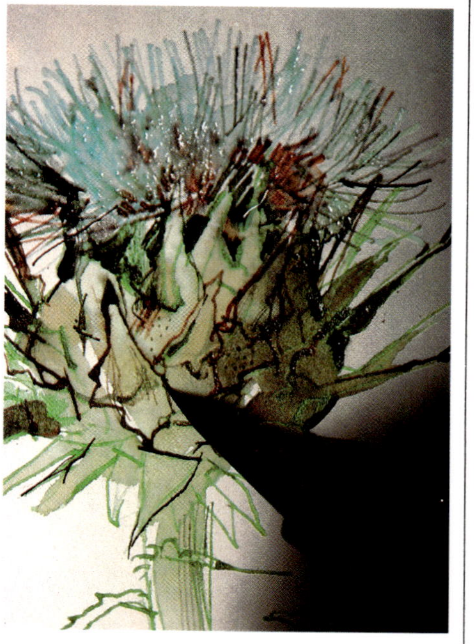

*With blue ink put in the shape of the flower, using quick directional strokes. Continue with black ink, working back over the lines already drawn in green. Do not attempt a smooth line, but allow the nib to catch on the paper* **(top left)**. *When the drawing is practically dry, mix a wash of light green and quickly block in the general colour areas* **(top centre)**. *Describe the final details of the thistle over the green wash* **(top right)**.

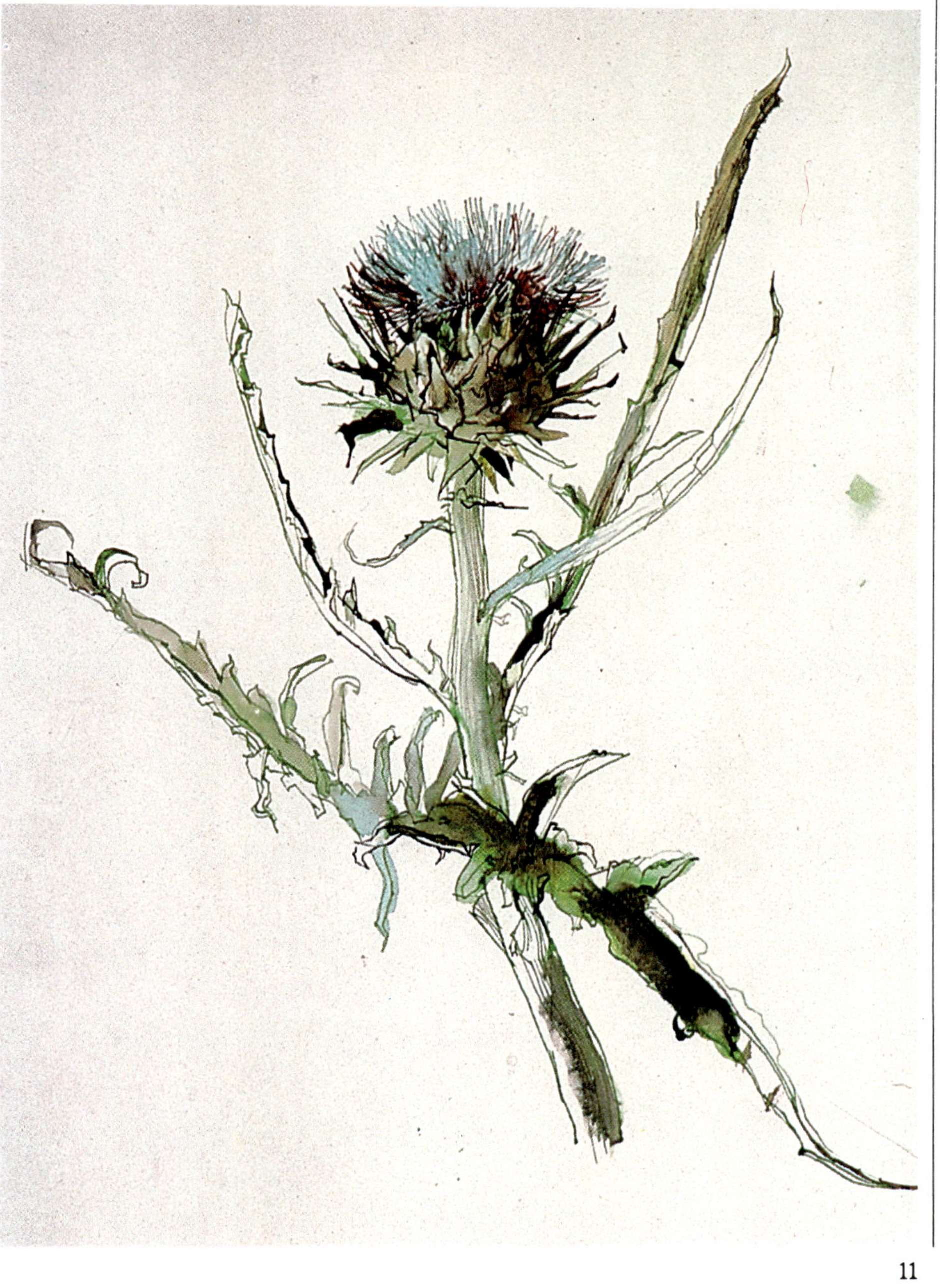

*Complete the drawing by working diluted blue shadows into the flower and by adding leaf shapes in clear, undiluted colour* **(right)**.

# RIVER SCENE WITH BRIDGE

Complex subjects such as this bridge demand a careful analytical approach on the part of the artist. A bridge is large with strong vertical and horizontal stresses and this sense of size and architectural space must be faithfully conveyed if the structure is to have conviction. It is essential to establish the correct scale and for the uprights to be parallel if the bridge is to look strong enough to carry the weight of vehicles or people.

There are two ways of effectively achieving these ends. Firstly, a grasp of simple perspective helps, and a relentlessly analytical eye is essential. The second approach is to draw what you 'see', not what you 'know' to be there — or rather what you think you know. Here the artist has used a combination of both to achieve a solid and structured drawing.

These pens make a fairly sharp and regular line, but with practice you will be able to achieve a wide variety of marks and textures. The nib is often rigid and stiff when new, but does wear down and soften with use. This particular artist uses several pens, using new ones when a sharp clear line is required, and saving the old one for laying softer, textured areas or for producing softer, less regular lines.

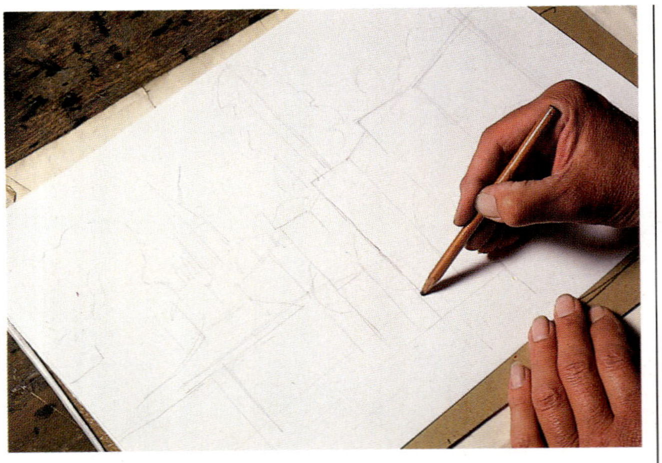

*When drawing a complicated structure such as a bridge, your first consideration should be to make the subject look convincing. Concentrate on the accurate positioning of the main structural lines, pencilling them in lightly to begin with* **(left)**.

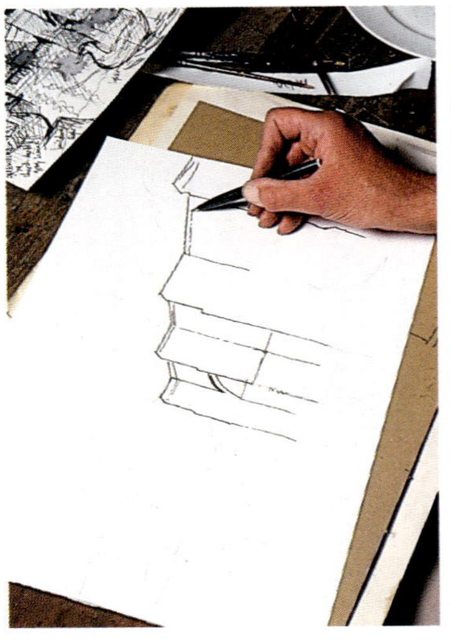

*Start to draw over the light structural guidelines with a felt nib pen, keeping the lines firm and simple* **(left)**.

*Add areas of shadow where this helps the form and character of the subject* **(below)**. *Very dark shadows can also be suggested to help establish the main areas of the composition.*

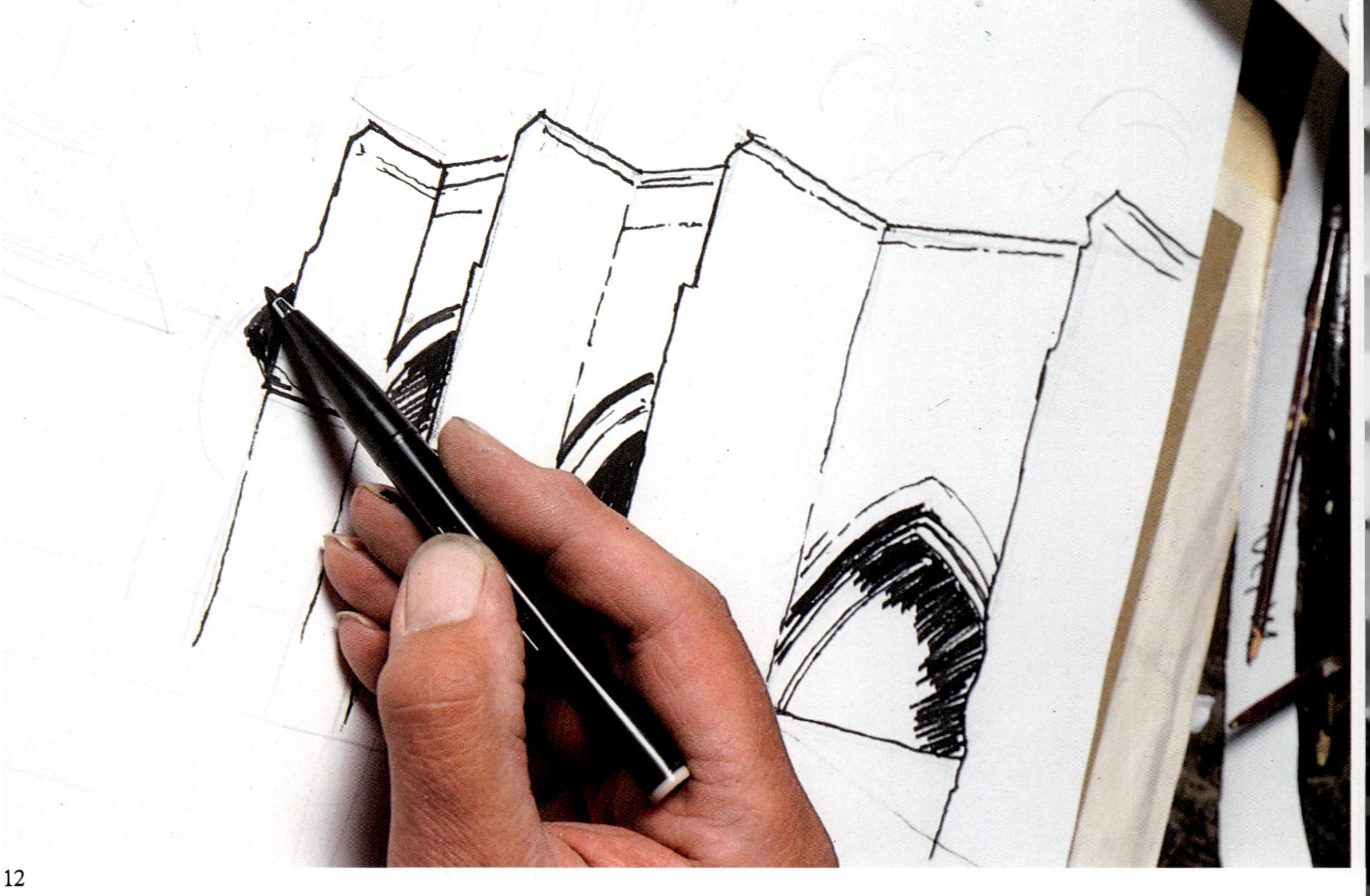

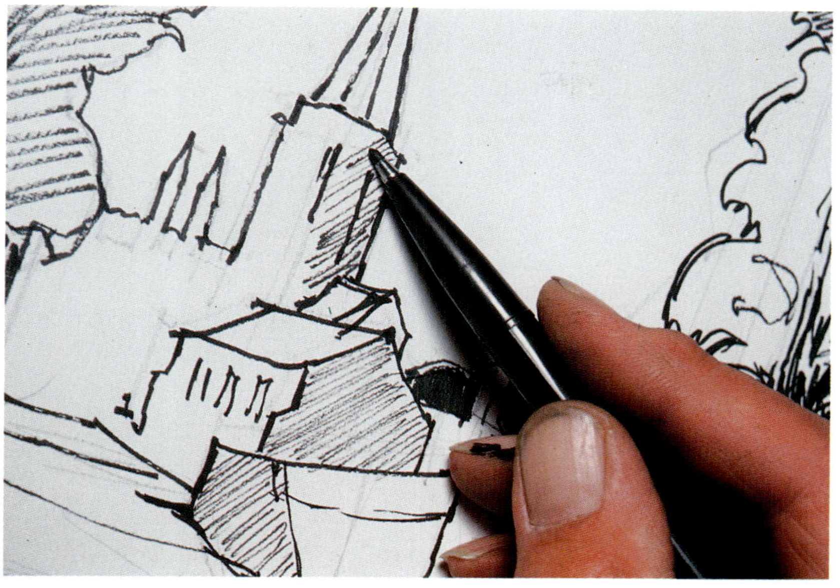

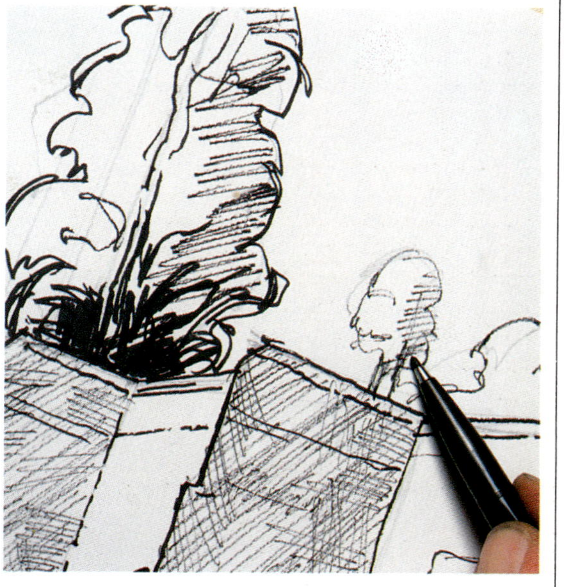

*Sketch in the outline of the background shapes, using a regular hatching stroke to describe shade* **(above)**.

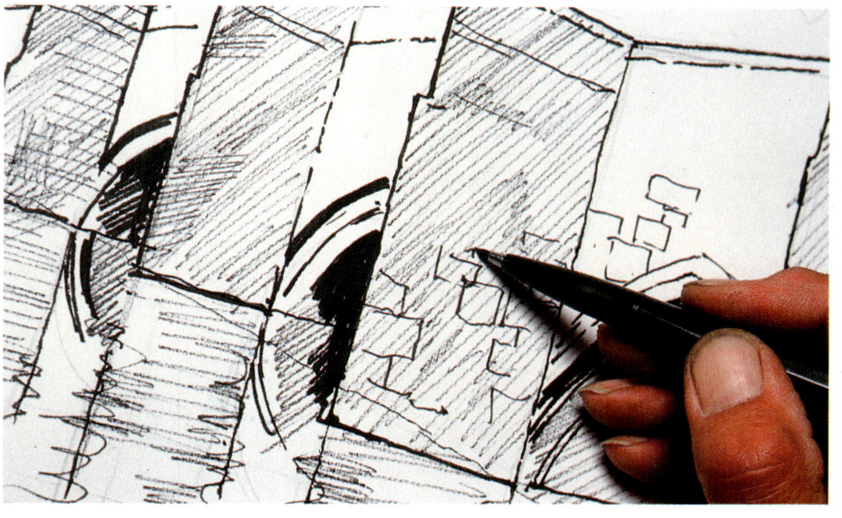

*Develop the tones in the drawing by working into the shadow areas. Use cross-hatching to define very dark shadows, working over this several times if necessary to obtain the required depth* **(above and left)**.

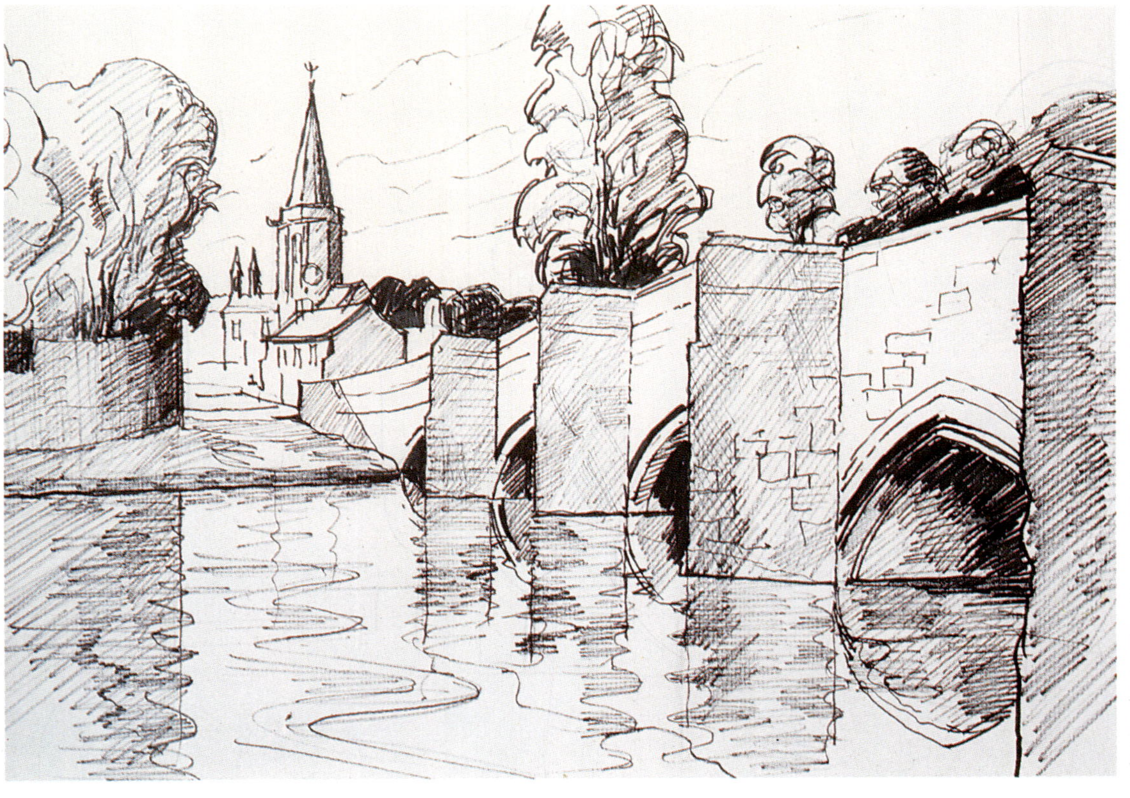

*Tackle large areas of stonework by drawing selected areas rather than attempting to fill in every single stone, and complete the drawing by adding strong reflections on the water surface* **(left)**.

# WOMAN SITTING

In this drawing the artist used a rapidograph rather than traditional pen and ink, preferring the more consistent, regular line which rapidograph produces. This enabled areas of fine cross-hatching to be developed without fear of the ink dripping or blotting. The white paper has been allowed to stand for the highlight areas. Areas of shade are described with cross-hatching.

Rapidographs can be demanding tools. You need a light touch and must hold the pen upright to keep the ink flowing. Use a good quality cartridge paper or paper with a smooth art surface, otherwise paper fibres will clog the nib. If you are unfamiliar with this type of pen practise making a series of marks to see how you can create different textural effects. Do not try to imitate the line created by an ordinary pen — you will not succeed, nor will you get the full benefit of the inherent qualities of the rapidograph. The artist has used a variety of outlines and shaded areas, creating a strong graphic effect which is particularly appropriate to this particular medium.

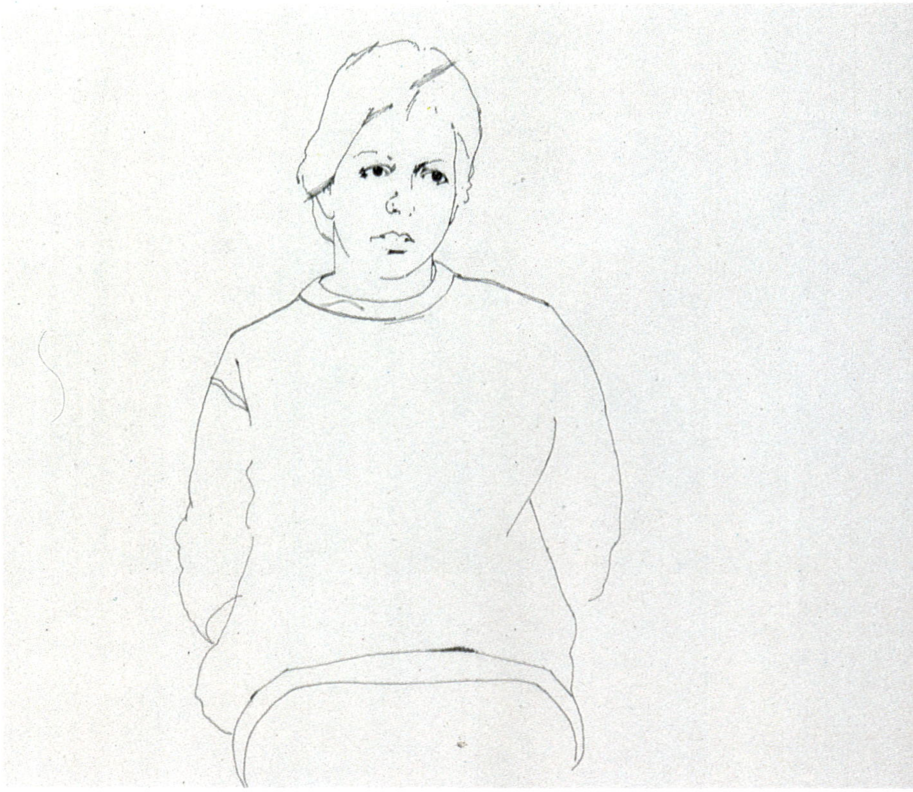

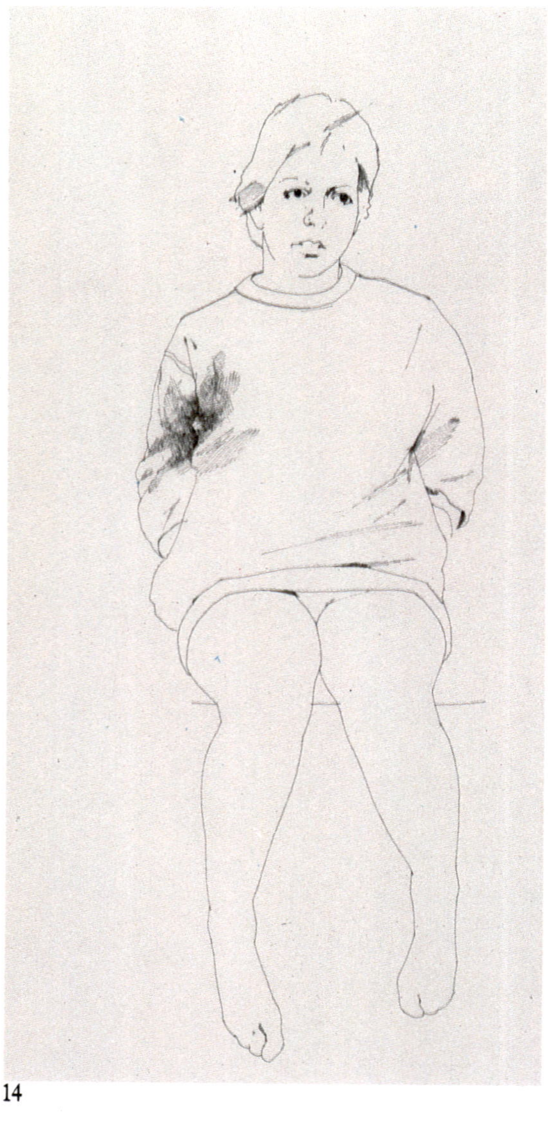

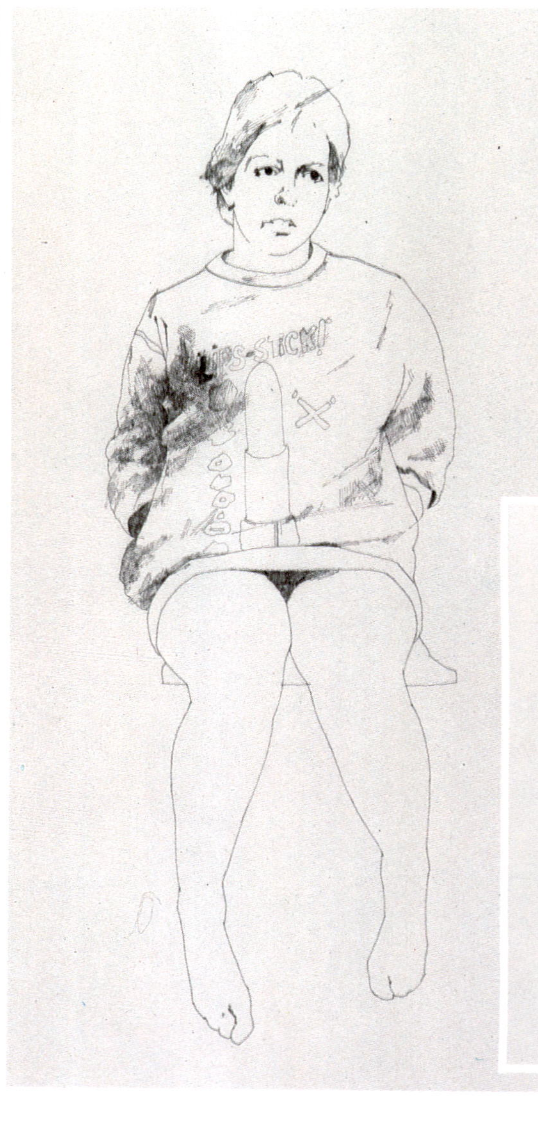

*Use a rapidograph for this portrait drawing, and work on good quality cartridge paper. Holding the pen almost upright to keep the ink flowing, start to draw in the outline of the subject* **(above)**. *Begin to develop the shadow area on the upper arm by lightly hatching and cross-hatching in small areas. Work the line in different directions* **(far left)**. *Draw into the figure and hair, developing other shadow areas* **(left)**. *Put in the dark areas of the seat with dense cross-hatching* **(below)**.

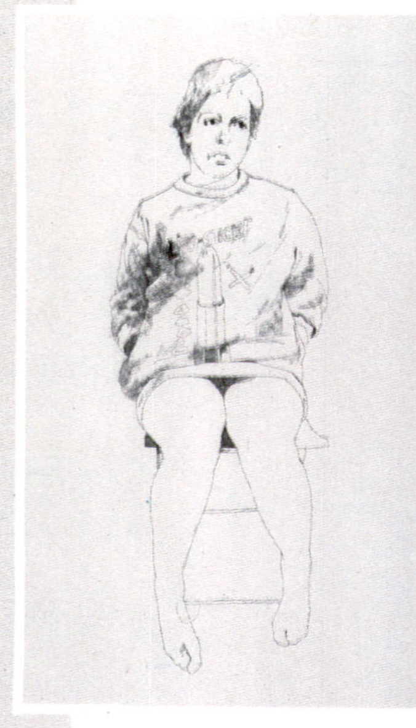

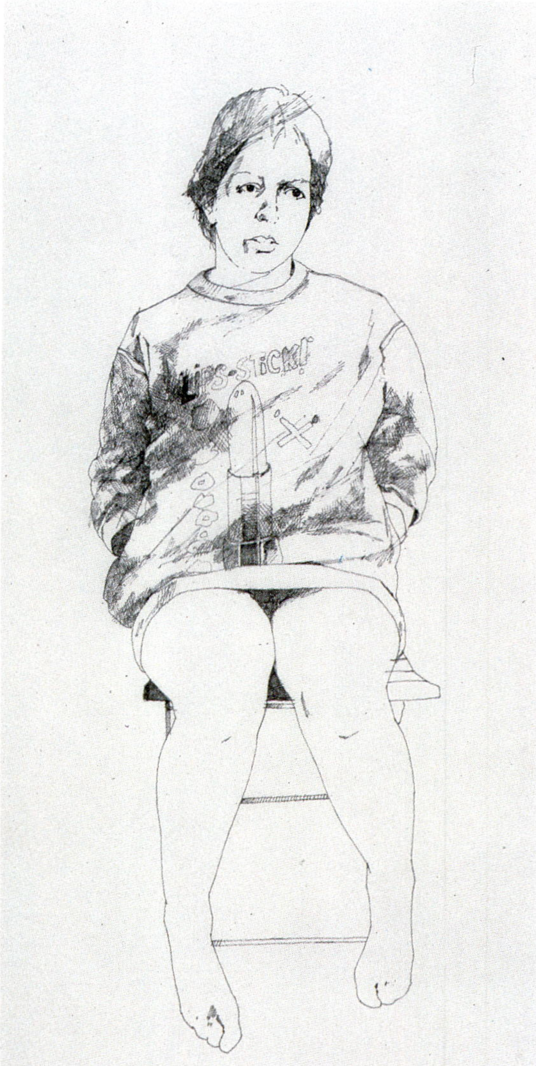

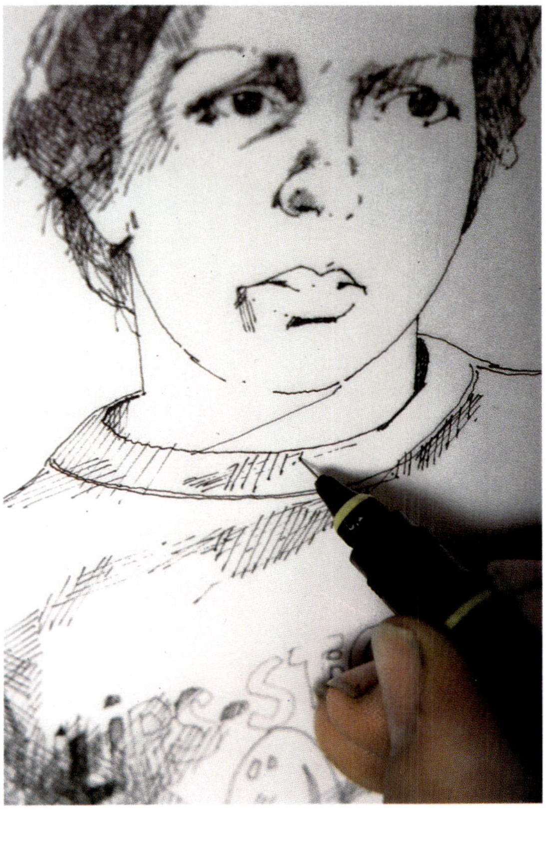

*Work into the face, and with a very light stroke put in the shadows around the nose and eyes* **(left)**. *Shake the pen frequently to make sure the nib does not clog. Use fine lines of cross-hatching to create subtle tones and small shadow areas* **(bottom left)**. *These delicate lines can be achieved by holding the pen in a sensitive way and applying very light, even pressure. To finish the drawing, continue to work on the shirt and head, heightening dark areas by overlaying strokes in different directions* **(below)**.

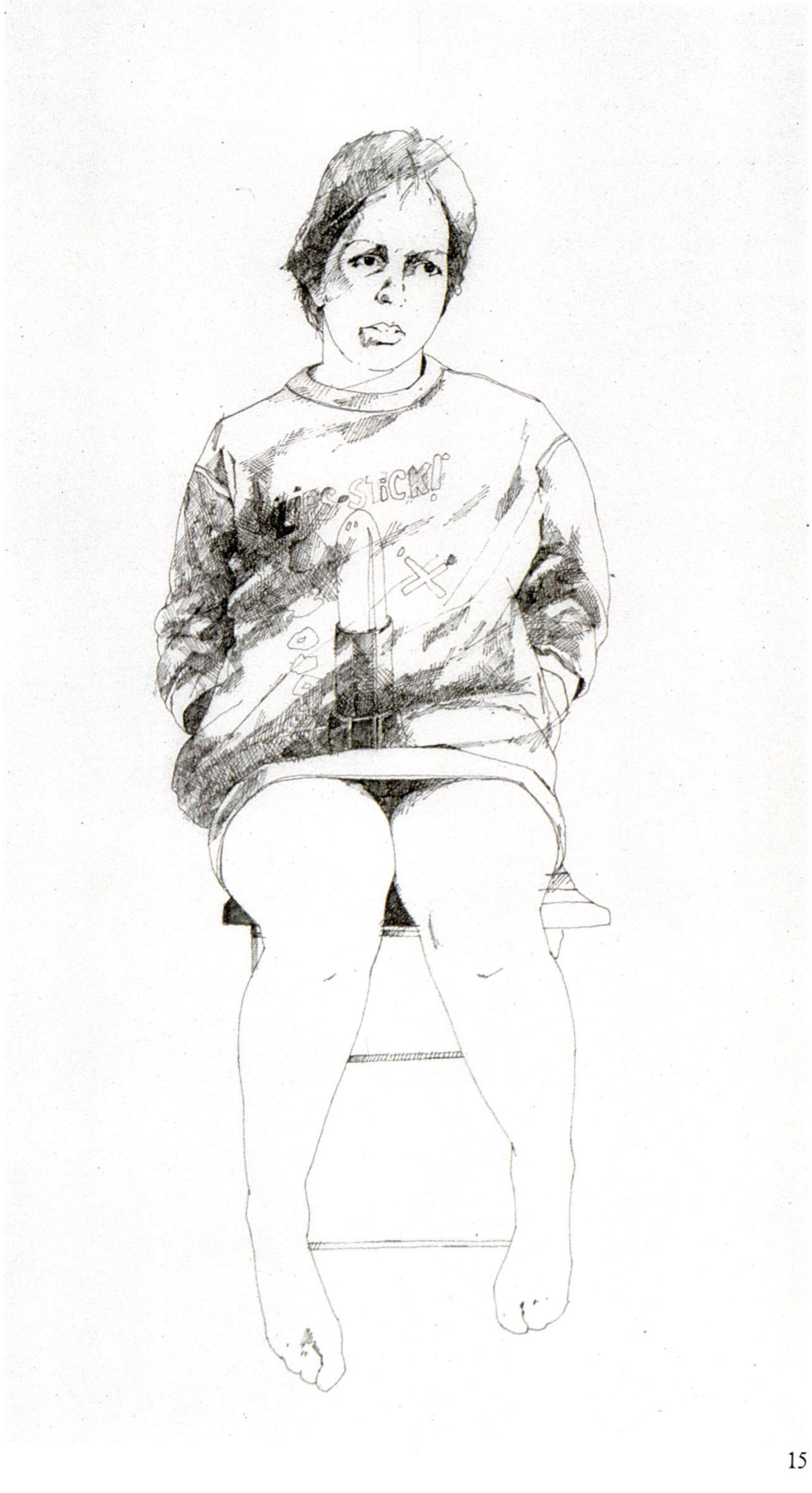

# NUDE SEATED

Although pen and ink may initially prove awkward to work with, you will soon develop a feel for the medium and be able to exploit the natural flow of the ink. The pen and ink artist creates a drawing using the white of the paper and the black of the ink, and creating many tones between the two extremes. These tones are usually created by the use of individual lines of ink which, when laid over one another in various directions, create a mesh-like effect giving an impression of shadow and depth. Unlike many other drawing and painting media the pen and ink artist is limited to the use of line alone for developing tone but — as this drawing demonstrates — highly modelled, accurate work is possible.

*Sketch in the figure very roughly with a 2B pencil, put in the general outlines in ink and begin to describe shadow areas* **(left)**. *Continue the outline of the figure and work into these putting in shadow areas. Use a hatching stroke to define muscles* **(bottom left)**. *Continue the outline of the arm* **(below)**. *Moving outside of the figure, very loosely put in broad strokes of background shadow, working in one direction* **(right)**.

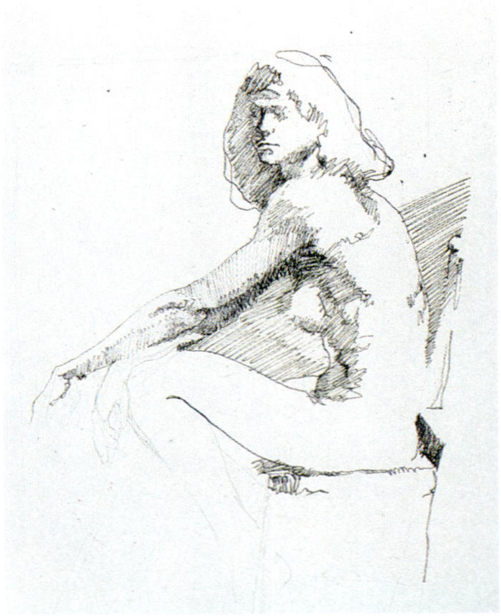

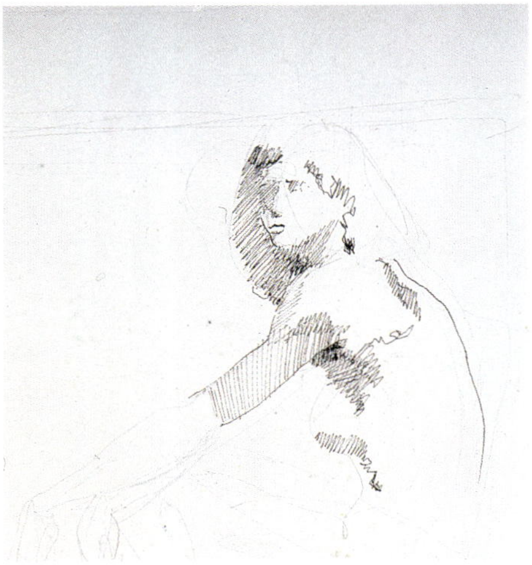

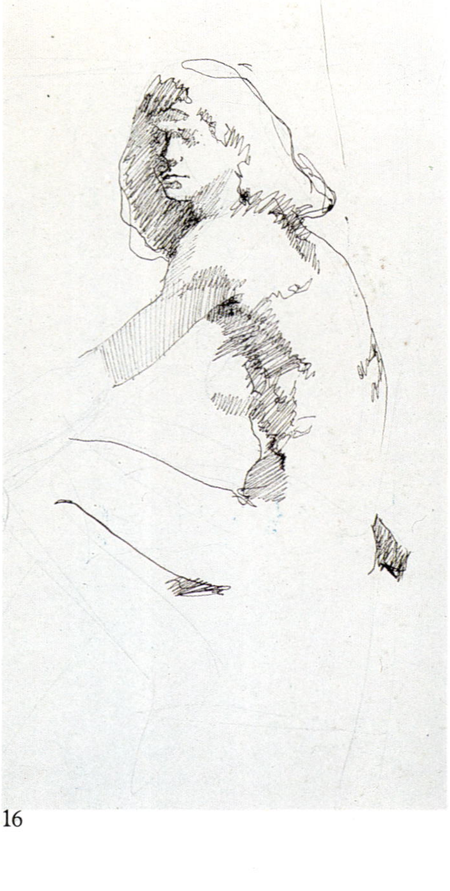

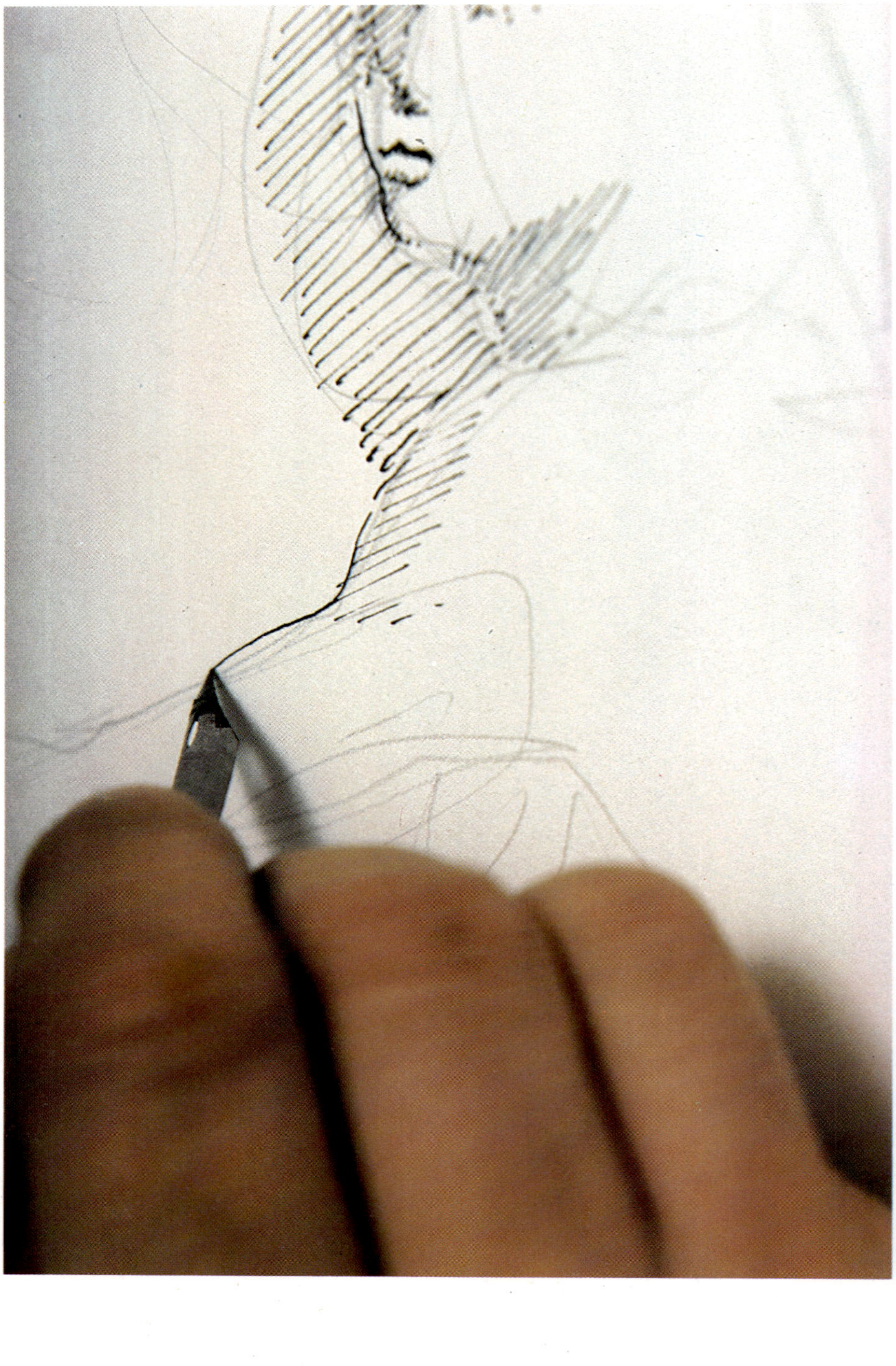

*Changing the direction of the line, put in general shadow over the leg. Cross-hatch over the background shadow to create a denser tone* **(right)**.

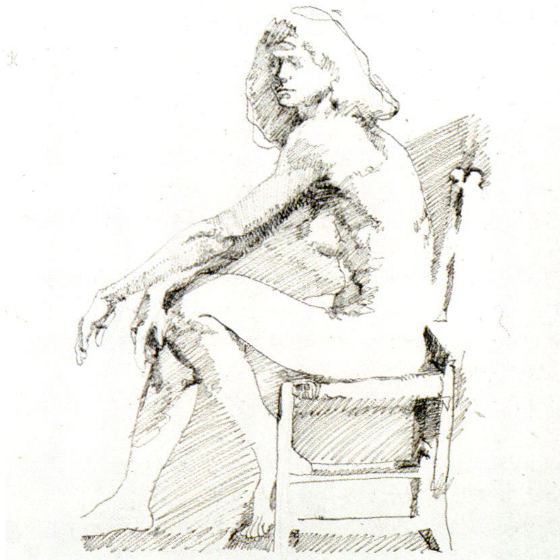

*Carry the background area down behind the chair using the same directional strokes. Leave areas of white paper to define the chair shape* **(below)**.

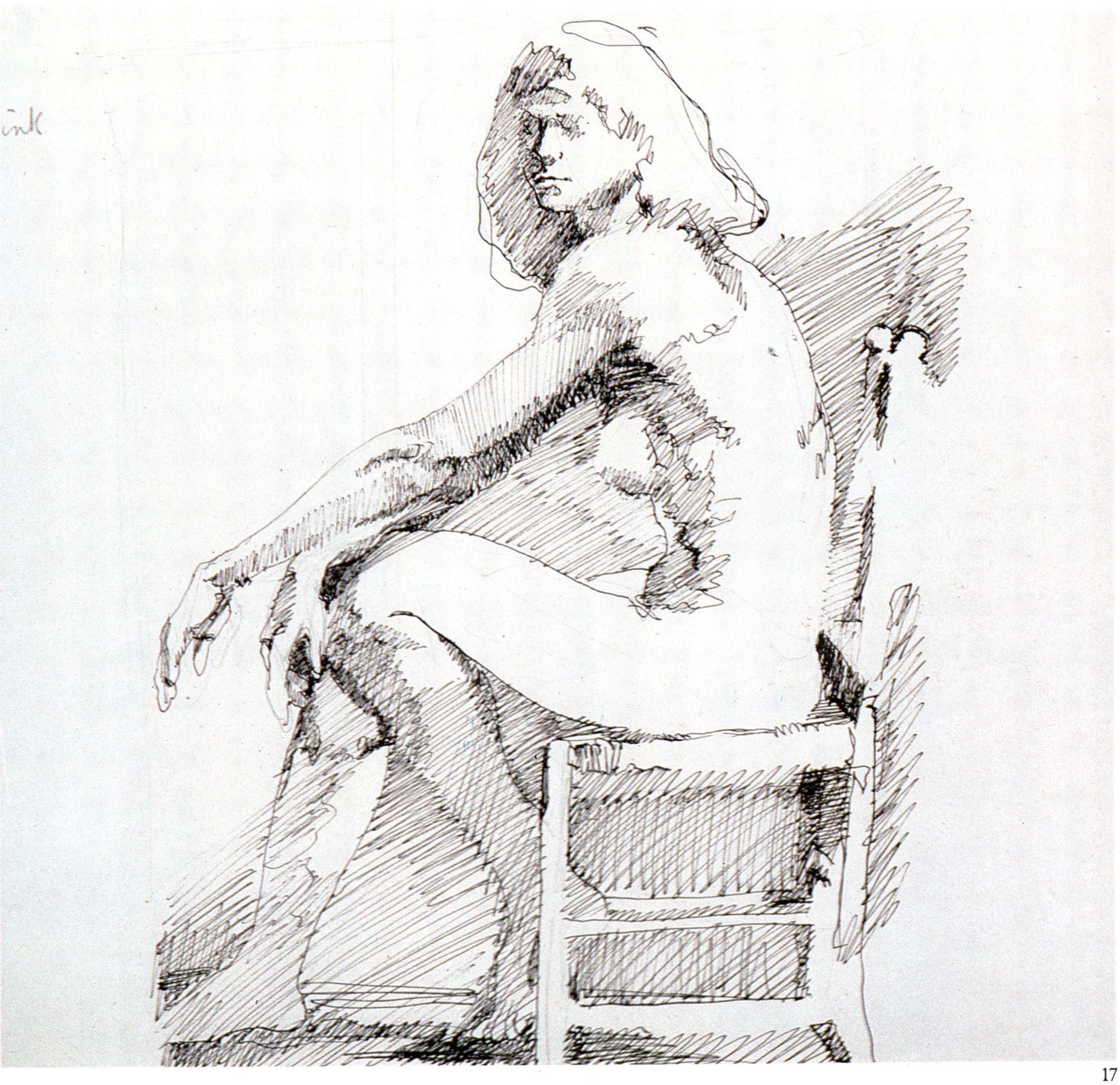

# STILL-LIFE WITH HAT

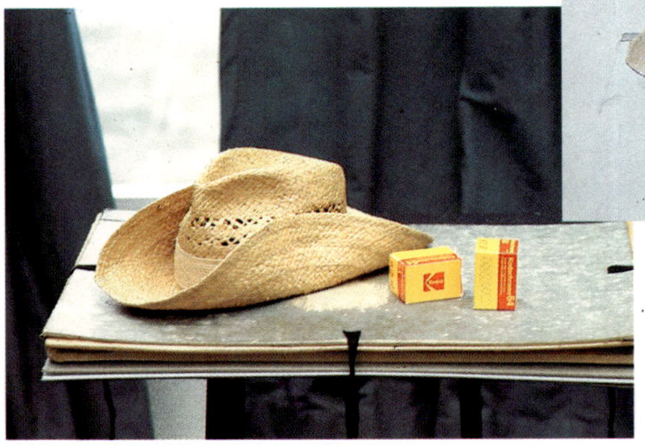

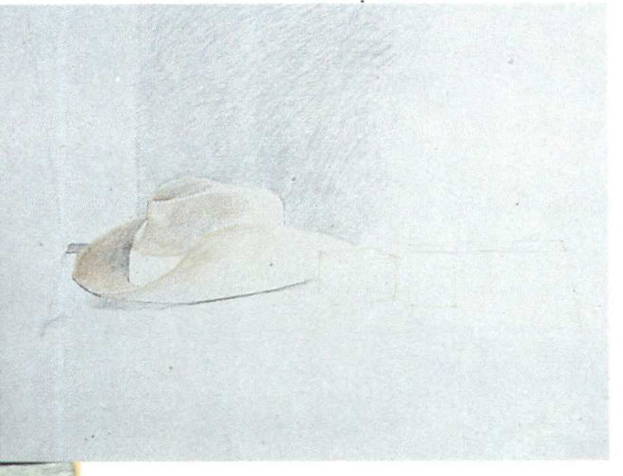

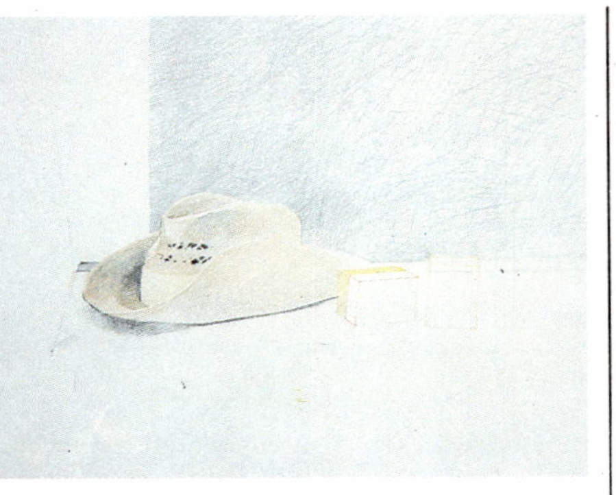

*Make a selection of objects randomly selected from whatever is to hand* **(top left)**. *Start by laying in a block of light blue shading behind the hat, varying the direction of the pencil strokes. Use the same blue for shadows on and around the hat* **(top centre)**. *Strengthen and broaden the background colour, developing the shadow and pattern details of the hat. Draw in the shape of the boxes with yellow and red pencils* **(top right)**.

*Create subtle colour variations by overlaying light pencil strokes, using warm and cool tones together* **(right)**. *Using a finely sharpened pencil, describe small detail areas in a darker colour* **(below)**.

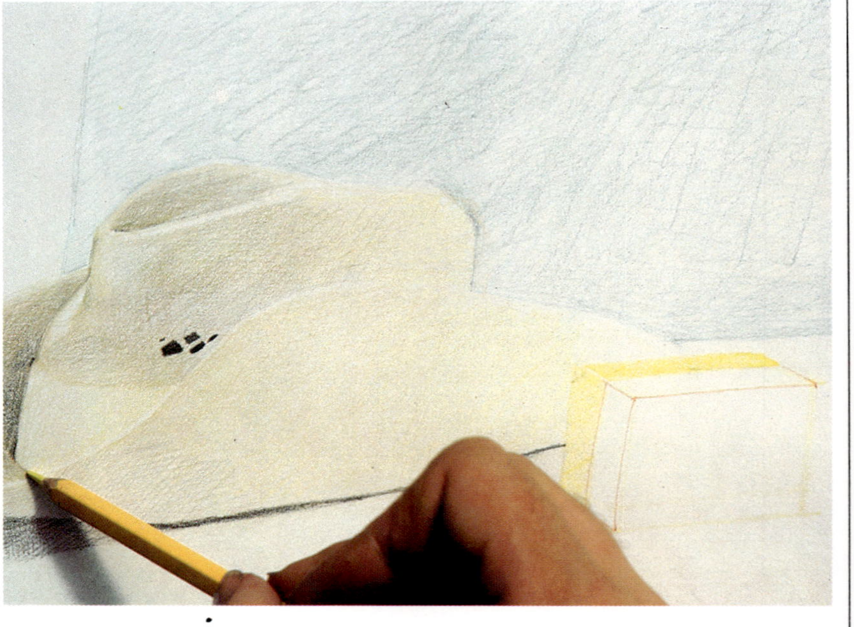

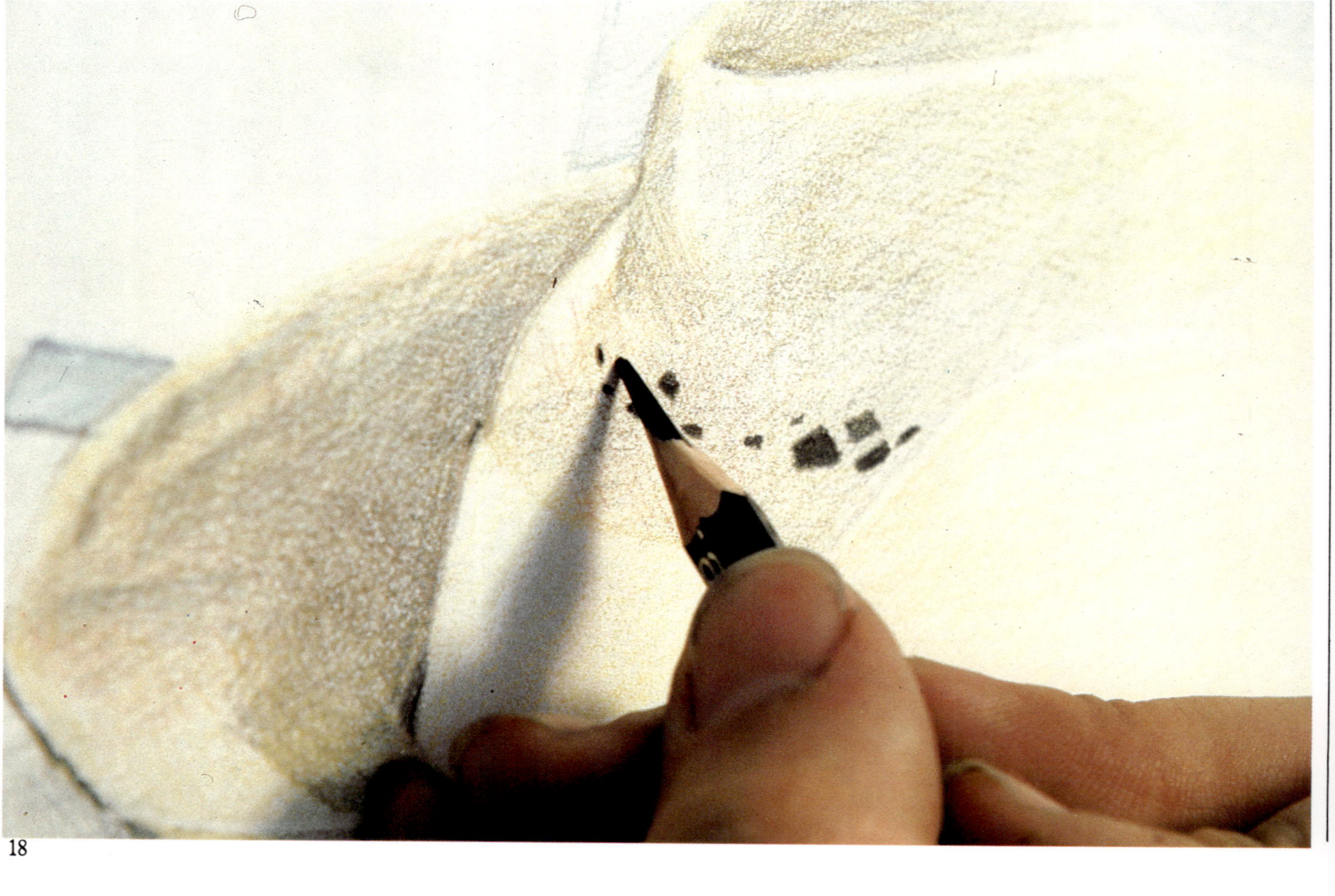

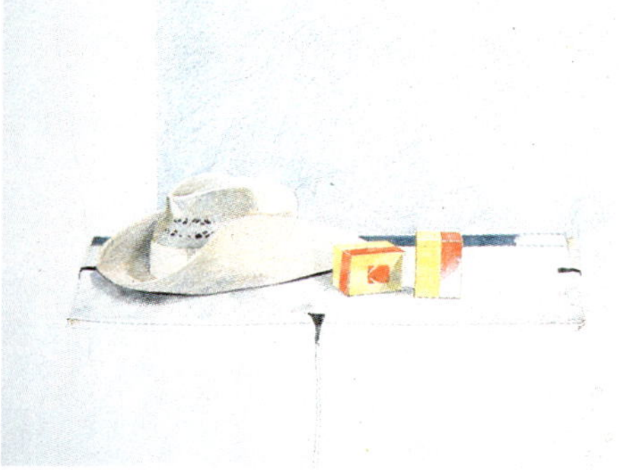

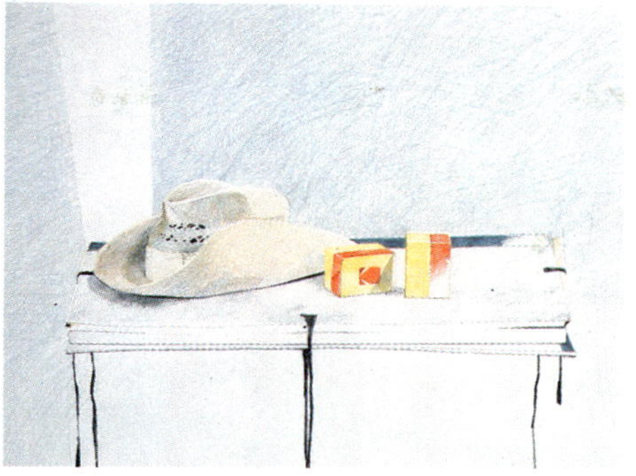

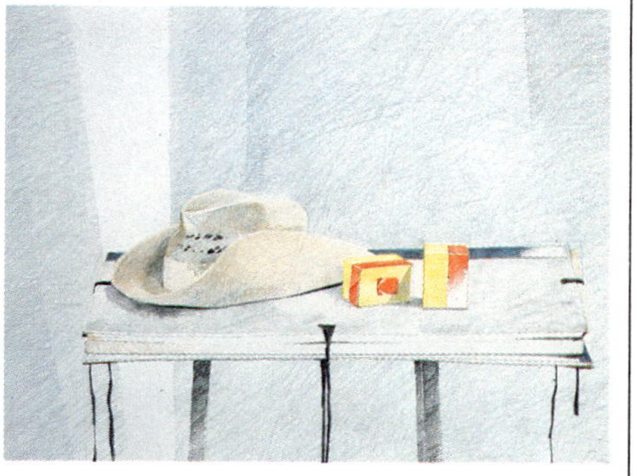

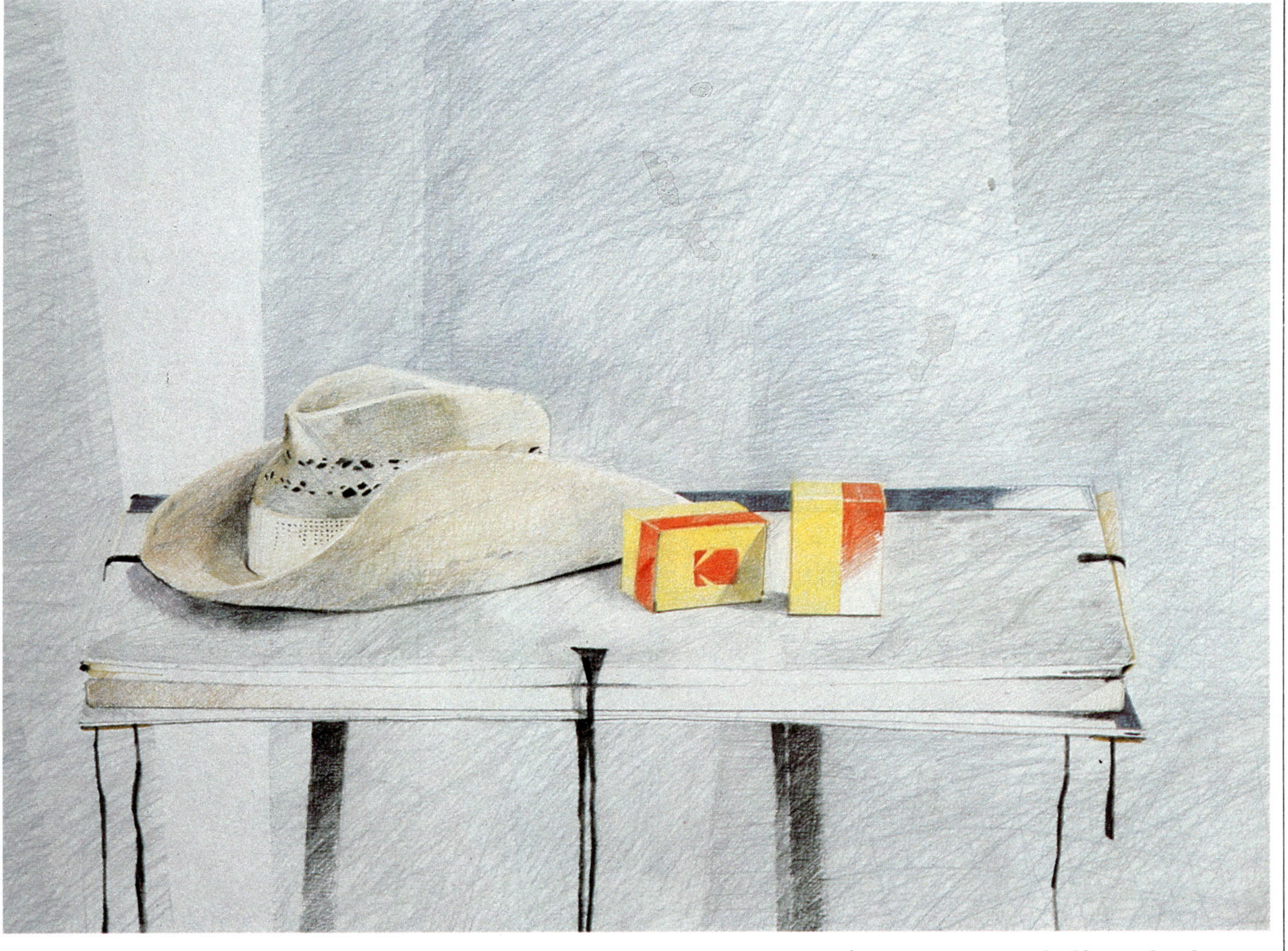

A still-life arrangement is an excellent opportunity to study form and colour in your own time, from an arrangement of objects of your own choice. Your subject may be a traditional one such as flowers and fruit, or it may be a random selection of things which are near to hand or which you particularly like. The artist chose these items for their simple colour range and the contrasting geometric and irregular shapes.

The delicate appearance of this drawing is created by successive overlaying of lines in different colours, which blend together to form a vast range of subtle hues. Each layer of colour is laid in light cross-hatching to gradually build up the finished effect. Purple and blue combine to give rich deep shadows on the yellows, echoing the colours of the background; red over yellow provides the rich shadow tone on the boxes.

Coloured pencils are waxier than traditional graphite pencils making them difficult to erase. This waxiness also tends to clog the paper if the colour is overworked. For this reason it is best to use the pencils lightly, never laying more than two or three colours over each other.

*Building up the colours with contrasts of tone. Use purple in the shadows under the hat, and darken the blues to make the objects stand out* **(top left)**.
*Outline the portfolio and sketchbook in black, and strengthen the bright colours* **(top centre)**. *Lay in the rest of the background area in blue, varying the tones with heavy reworking. Build up the details of line and tone with black and yellow ochre* **(top right)**. *The finished picture shows how coloured pencils can create a subtle yet clearly defined image.*

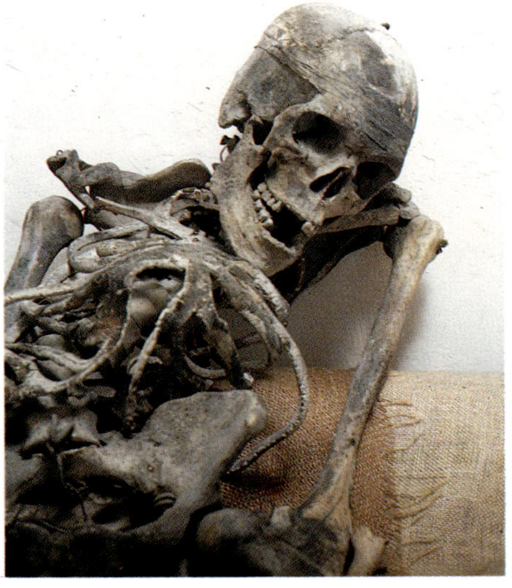

# HUMAN SKULL

A human skull is an ideal subject for a pencil drawing. It has a fluid and well defined outline as well as a variety of linear and tonal detail within its complex form. The smooth, rounded dome of the skull demands subtle changes of tone which contrast with the dense black shadows in the sockets of the eyes, nose and mouth.

The forms are described by overlaid layers of cross-hatching; crisp, delicate lines outline the shapes and depict the small characteristics of the surface. Allow the image to emerge gradually by first developing the structure as a broad view of the whole shape and then breaking down each area to show details.

Take this opportunity to look closely at the shape of the skull. Knowledge of the underlying structure of the face will stand you in good stead and is invaluable when painting and drawing portraits. The cranium, the larger part of the skull, is almost egg shaped. The bones of the face which influence the surface appearance are the nasal bones, the cheekbones, the two upper jawbones and the lower jawbones. Viewed from the front, over a third of the area of the skull is taken up by the frontal bone of the cranium. Beneath this, and separated by the nasal bones, are the eye sockets, or orbits. These are deep cavities, the margins of which are rectangular with rounded edges. The lower orbital margins are made up by the cheekbones and upper jawbones. The lower jawbone is jointed to the cheekbone at the point where it meets the temporal bone at the side of the cranium.

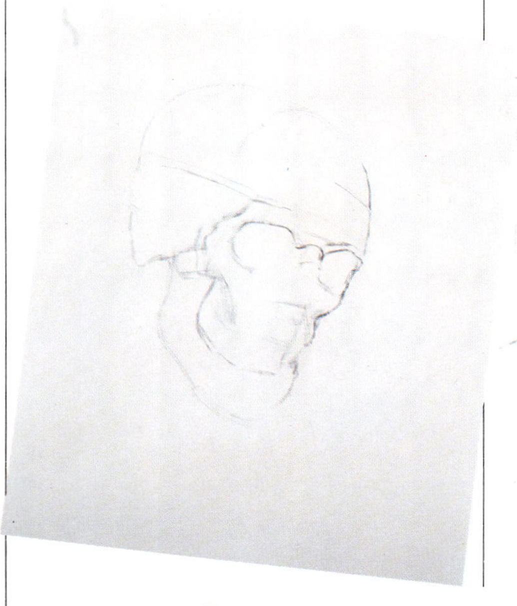

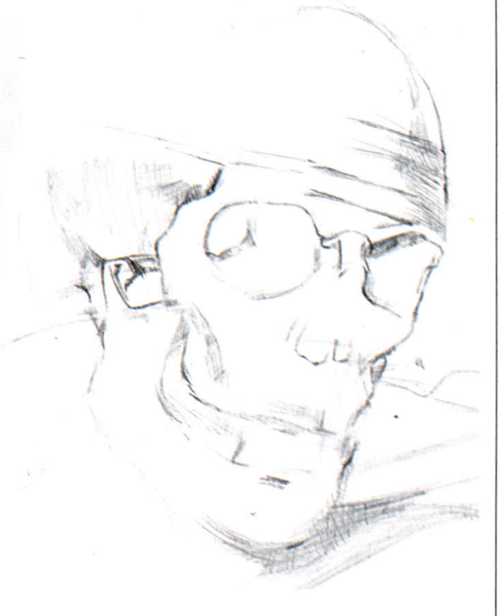

*Use pencil to capture the sharp, fluid outline of the skull and the sockets of the eyes and nose, working loosely with line and light hatching* **(far left)**. *Extend the outline and start to hatch in darker shadows* **(left)**. *Develop the drawing by blocking in small shapes and improving the definition of the contours* **(below left)**. *Continue to build up the drawing in more detail, drawing small shapes of the teeth and jaw socket* **(below)**. *Use an eraser where necessary to make corrections.*

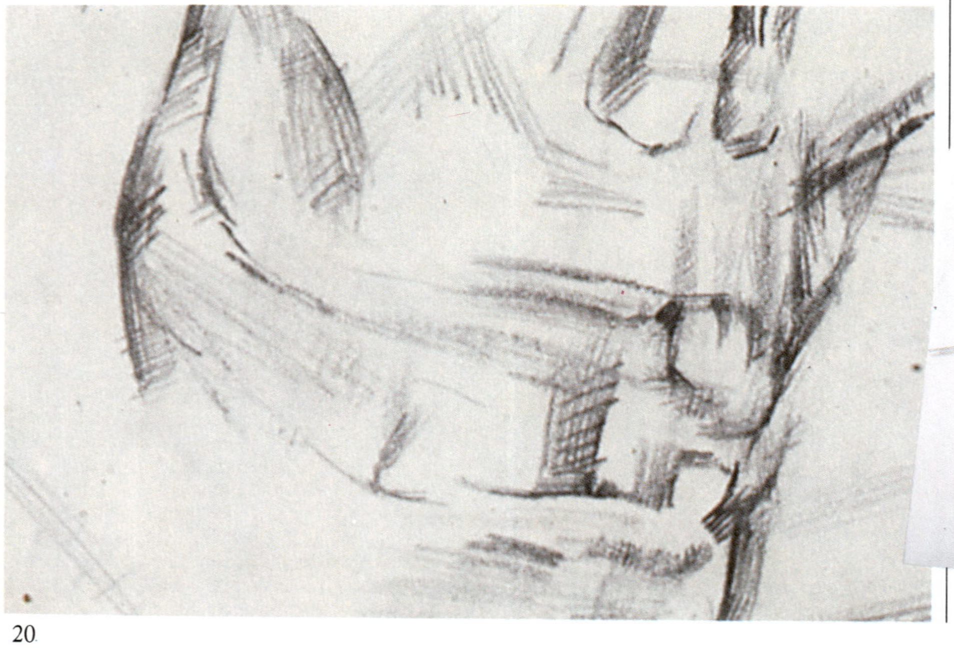

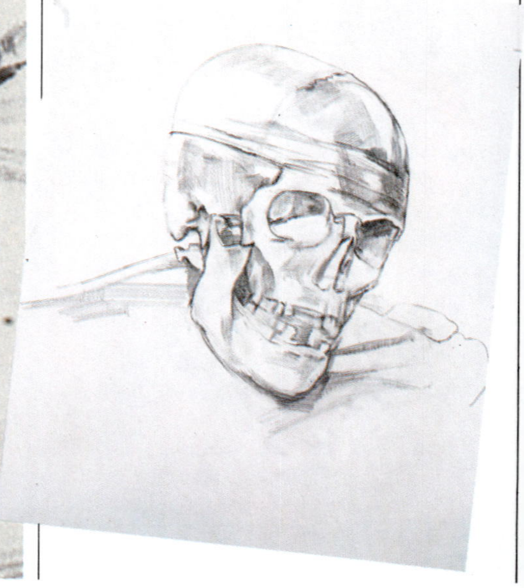

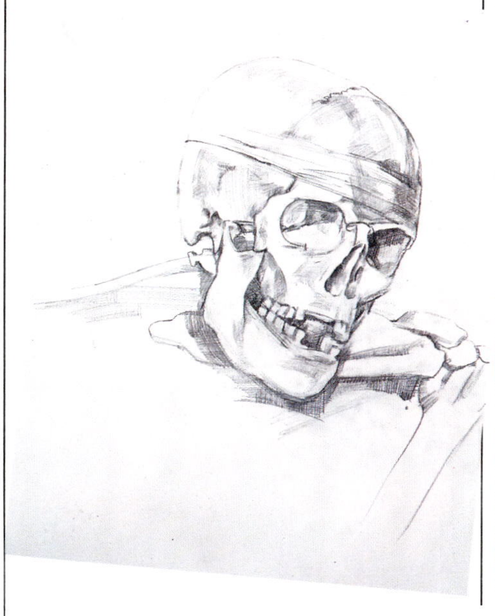

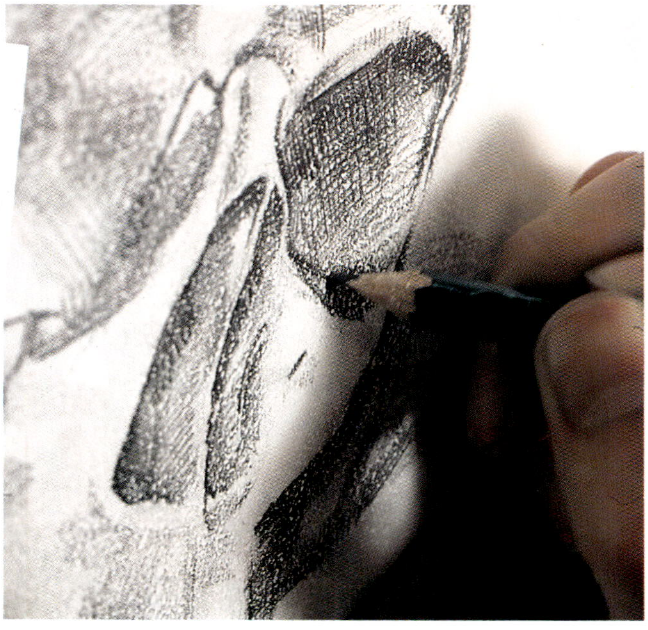

*Strengthen the outline and work over dark tones with cross-hatched lines to give depth and to bring out the full volume of the form* **(far left)**. *Continue to use cross-hatching to increase the shadow depth* **(left)** *— the darker the hatching, the more the shape will appear to recede.*

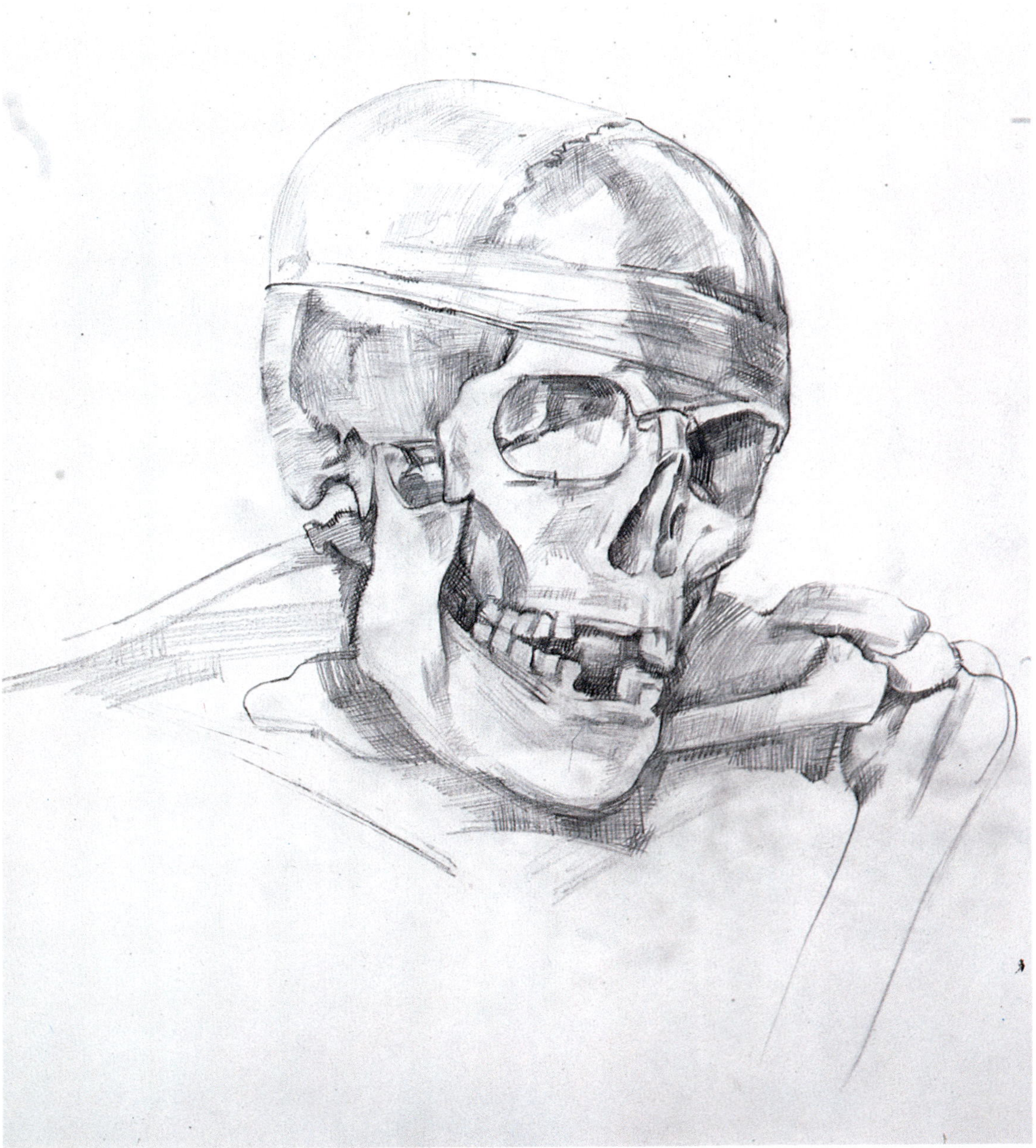

*Work across the whole image making minor adjustments to the tonal balance and reinforcing the lines where appropriate to clarify the overall structure of the finished picture* **(left)**.

# URBAN SCENERY

The stark lines of the modern urban landscape, interspersed with the mellower and more weathered shapes of older buildings, can provide the artist with a challenging and varied series of subjects.

Styles of draughtsmanship here can vary dramatically. On the one hand, you can use techniques which are almost identical with those of an architect, with a carefully measured approach and precise mathematical lines. Alternatively, the classical methods of drawing, concentrating on subtle differences of tone and using a more organic approach, can be extremely effective.

Just because you are drawing buildings, often embellished with such tiny components as windows and bricks, you should not be deterred from seeing the main, overall shapes and masses of a structure. You are still free to approach the drawing in any way you wish. The drawings on this page show that it is possible to look at buildings in an illustrative way, taking and developing those aspects which appeal to you personally; or you can take in an overall scene — observing how the volumes of the buildings and other angular shapes relate to each other and produce abstract shapes in the sky and background.

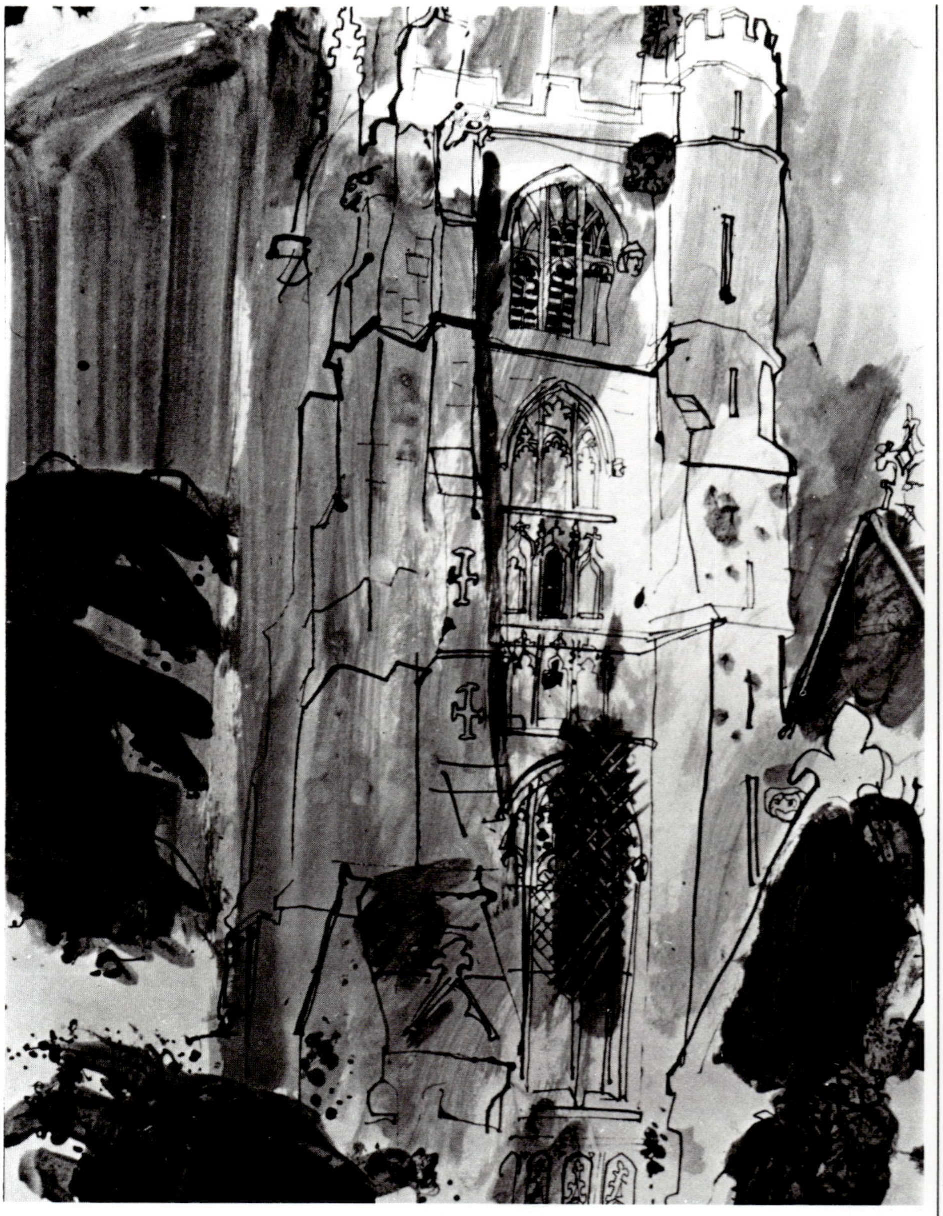

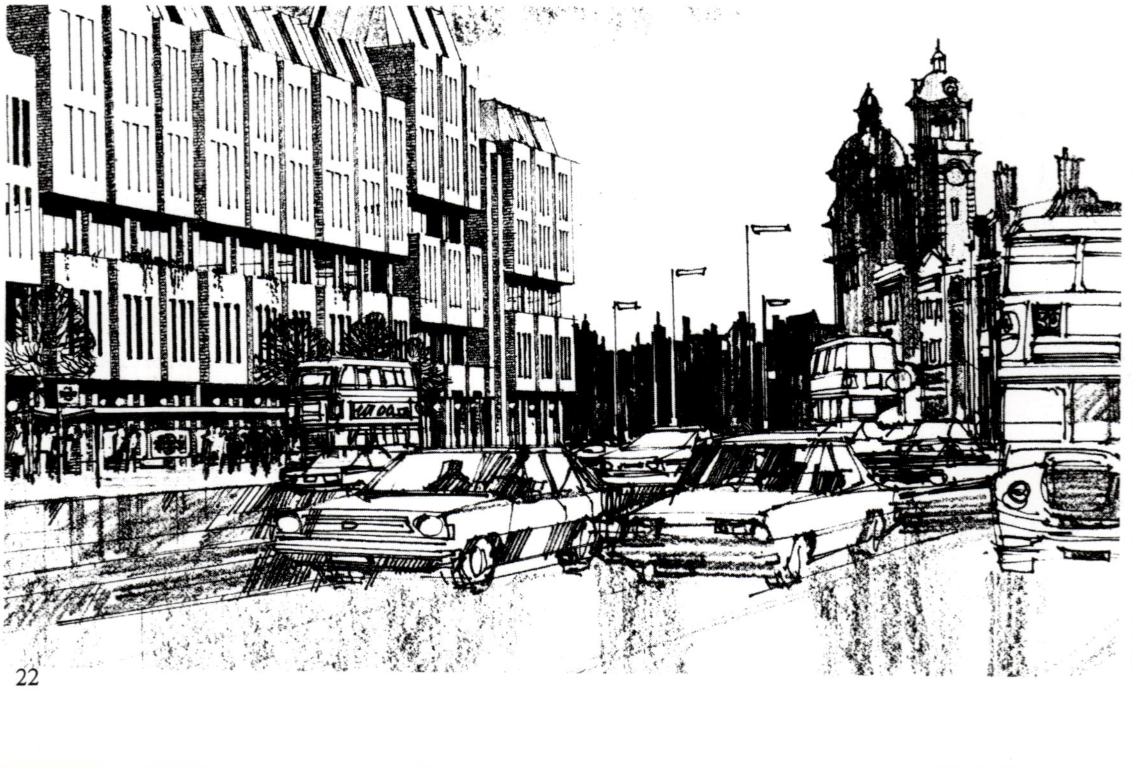

*In this imaginative drawing the artist has used a combination of ink and pastels. The architectural lines have not been allowed to dominate. Instead, the artist has used his own characteristic drawing technique, with lines of varying width, flowing free rather than straight, and brought to life by areas of contrasting light and shade* **(above).**

*The architect's impression* **(left)** *is in stark contrast. Buildings are precisely observed and mechanically executed.*

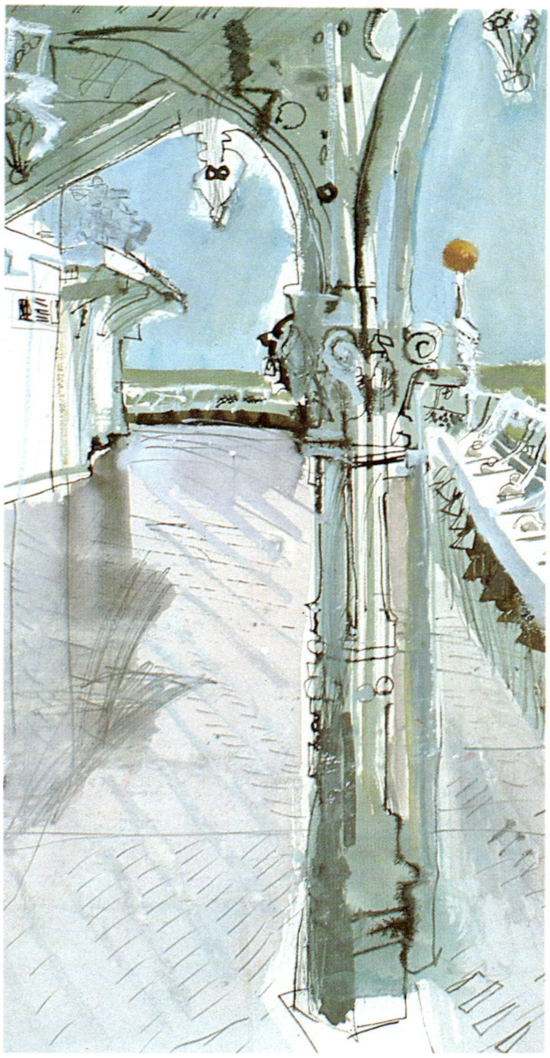

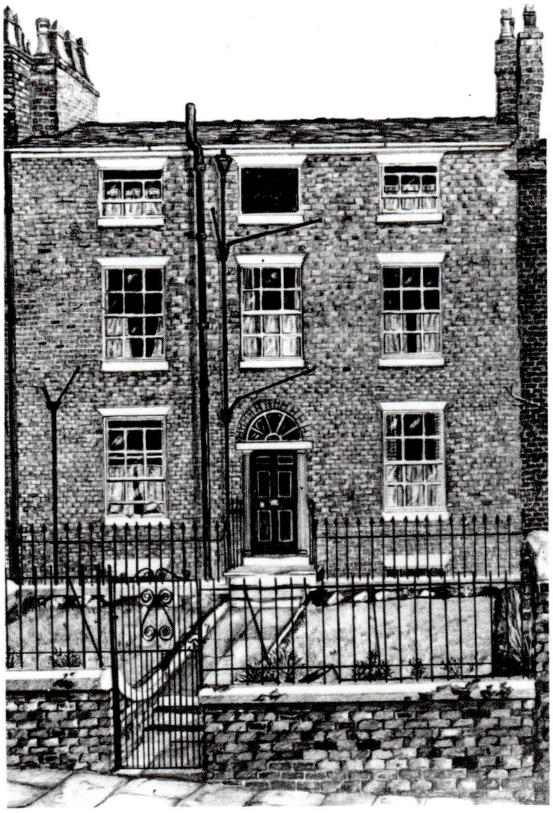

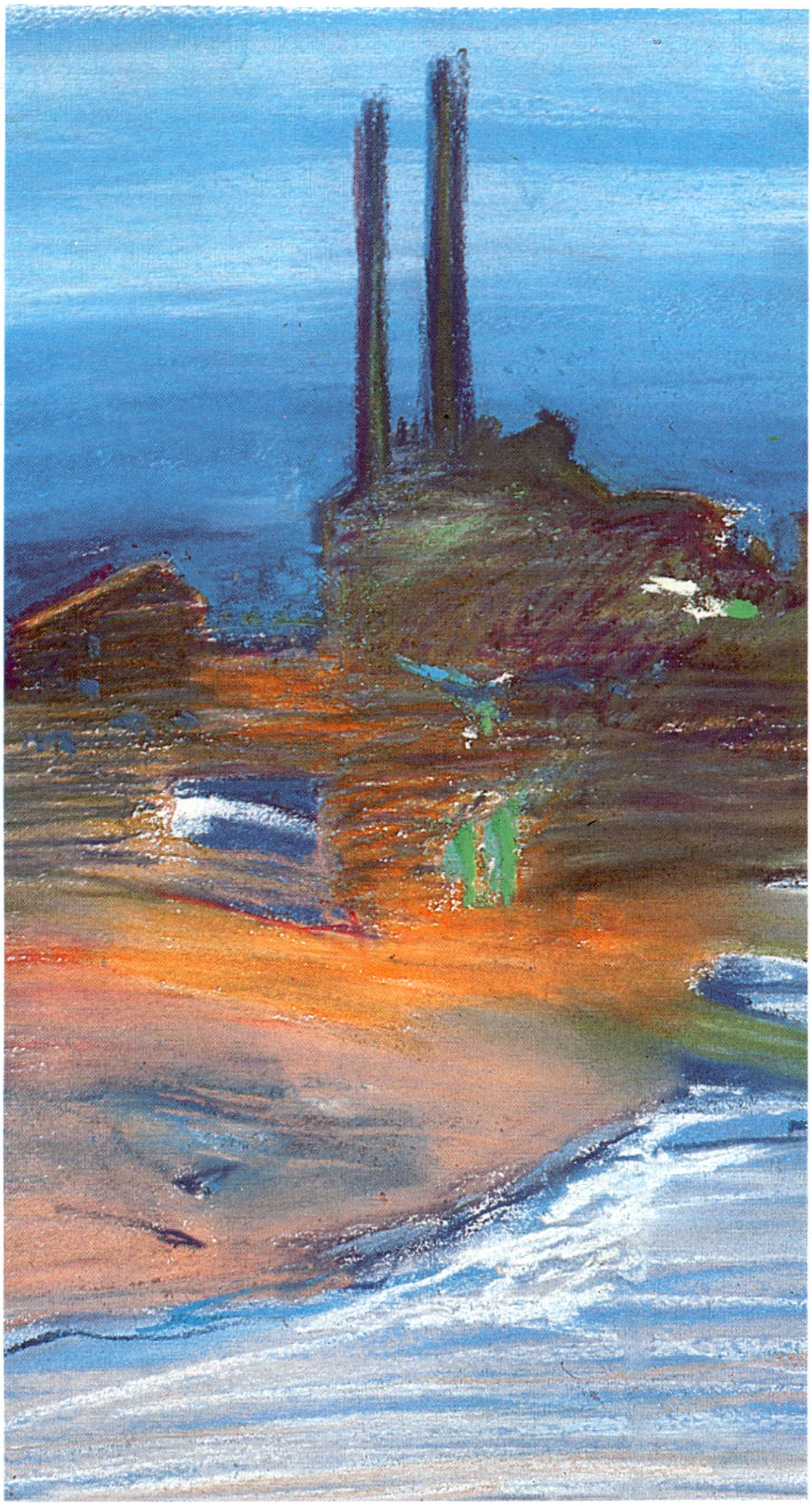

*The wrought-iron pillar of the isolated seaside pier* **(top left)** *inspired this ink and wash drawing. The artist recorded this architectural detail for inclusion in a painting at a later date.*

*The house* **(left)** *demonstrates the confusion of surface patterns such as the bricks, window panes, iron railings and roof tiles, which confront the urban landscape artist.*

*In this atmospheric oil pastel sketch* **(above)**, *the artist has ignored all detail and embellishment. His chief concern was the moody presence of the factory on the horizon.*

# SKETCHING IN THE COUNTRYSIDE

All the drawings on this page are from the artist's portfolio and were made with a view

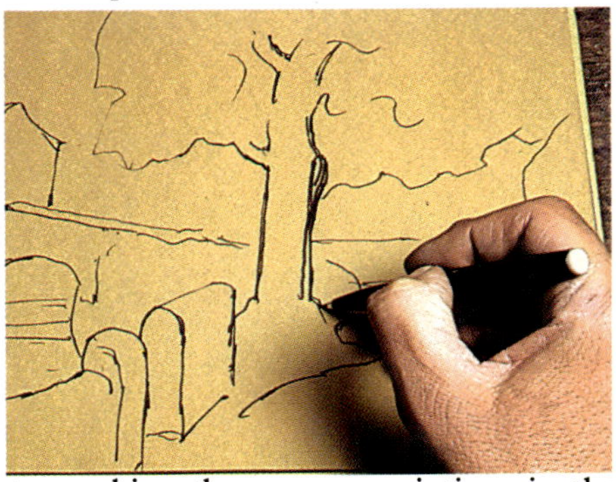

to working them up as paintings in the studio at a later date.

Before he started the drawings, the artist sat for some time looking at the subject in each case. He did this before even making a single mark on the paper. This kind of concentrated consideration will often surprise you, for even the most familiar subject will reveal new interest and your drawing will benefit immensely. For the artist, looking and 'seeing' is as important, or more important, than the marks he makes.

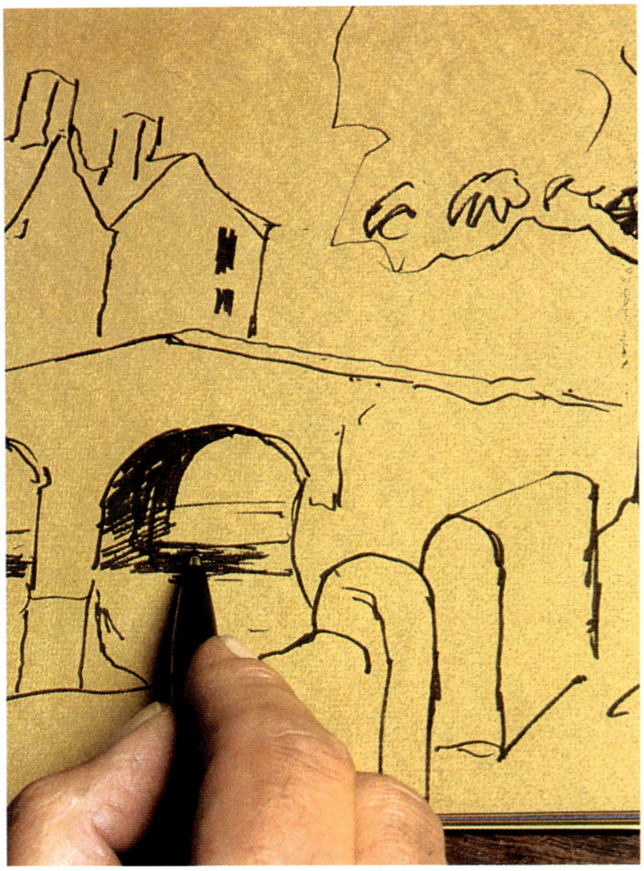

*Block out the general composition of the drawing* **(far left)**, *varying the line to suit the subject. Landscape sketching calls for greater versatility than most subjects — buildings, trees and water all requiring a different approach and sensitive treatment. Working across the whole sketch, introduce dark tone into the deepest shadow areas* **(left)**. *Use regular diagonal hatching to develop the medium tones, and a free, irregular stroke for the tree foliage* **(below)**.

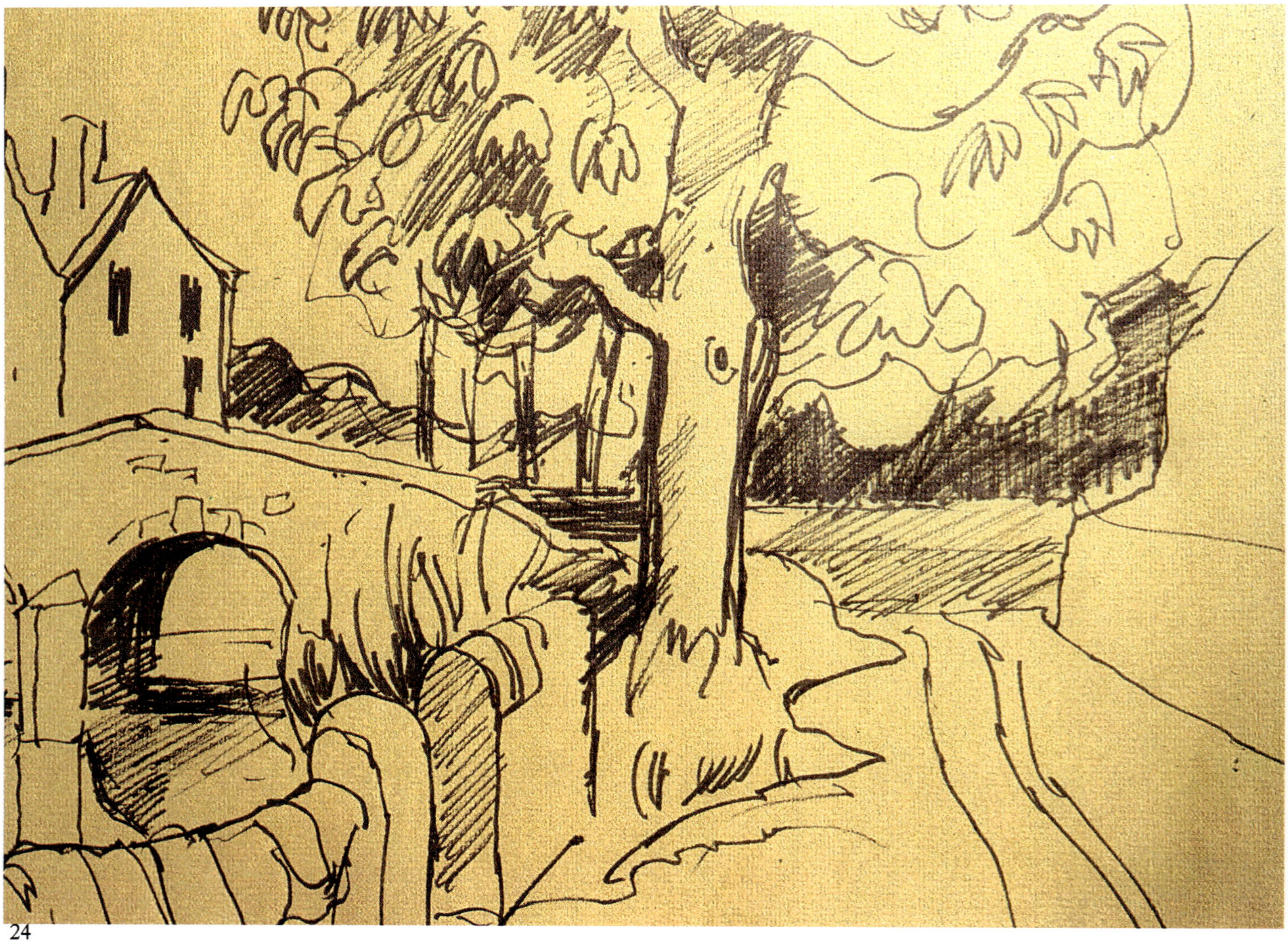

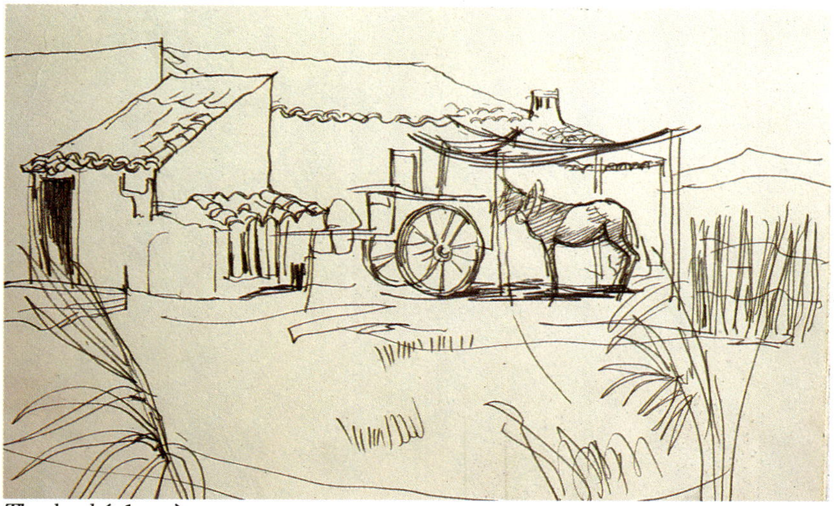

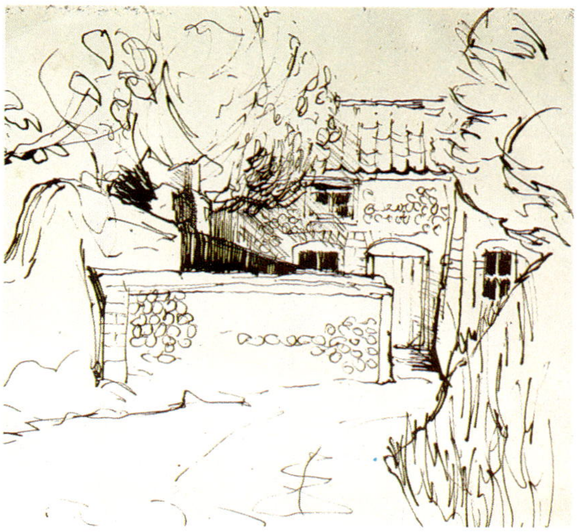

*The sketch* **(above)** *uses the minimum amount of information to record a passing moment on an isolated farm. The artist has accurately placed the waiting mule in its everyday setting by suggesting the layout of buildings, path and windswept trees. Simple perspective and a straightforward composition combine to convey the atmosphere of this undulating rural scene* **(right)**.

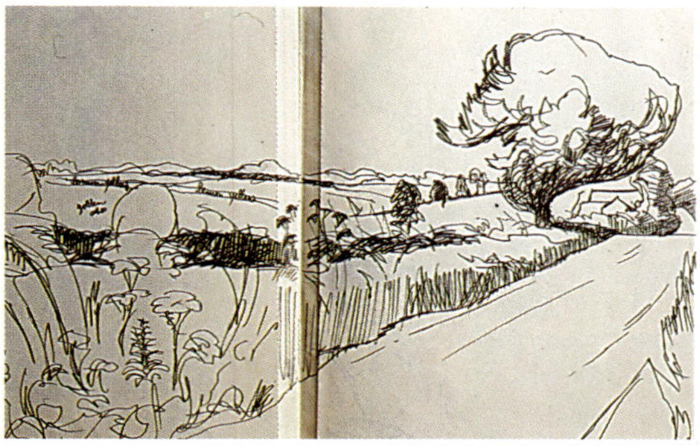

*The subject chosen here* **(above)** *has allowed the artist to relate the farm buildings to the shaded foliage behind. The barn, drawn in delicate line, is thrown into silhouette by the surrounding hatched tones.*

*Strong shading and the repeated image of the reflections in the water lend a feeling of coolness and tranquility to this riverside scene* **(below)**.

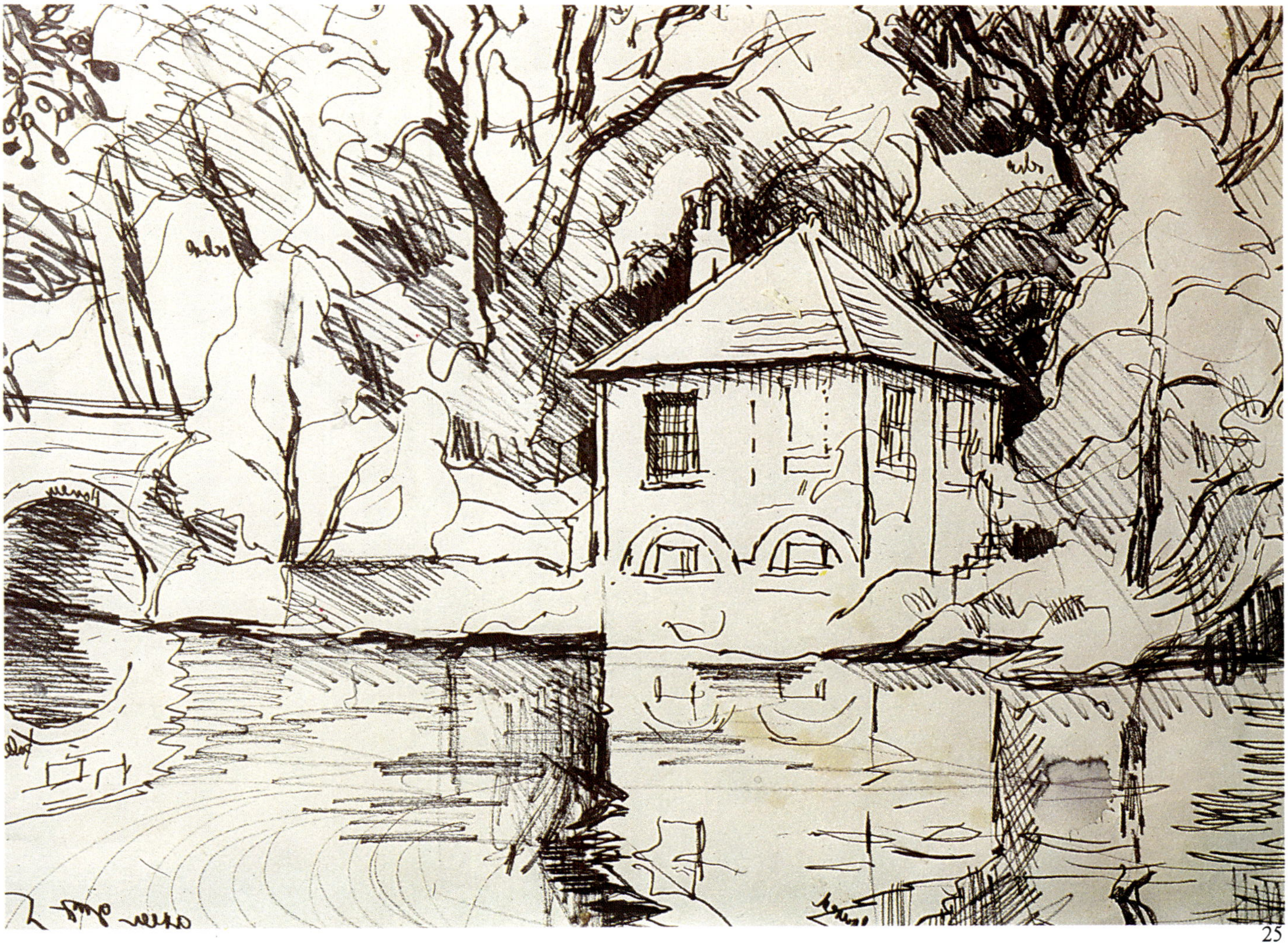

# THE RED BOOTS

Liberties have been deliberately taken with this subject, to give added life to a pair of old red boots. The artist has taken the general shape, composition, and colour of the subject and through an individual use of line and colour washes has exaggerated features to make the picture more descriptive. The techniques used are washed-in colour, line, and cross-hatching, juxtaposed to create an interesting combination of textures.

One important aspect of this drawing is the use of negative space to define details.

1

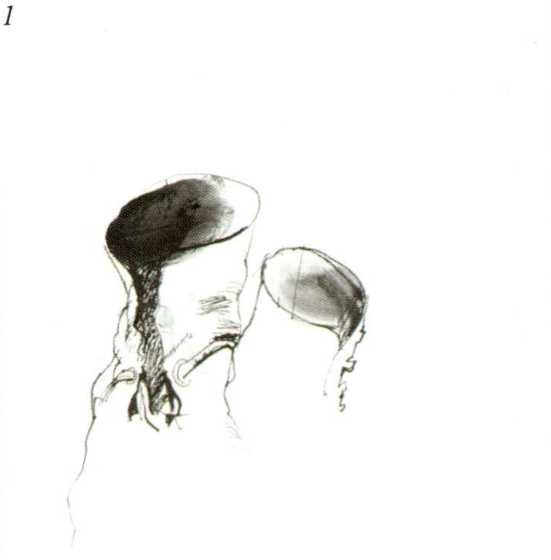

2

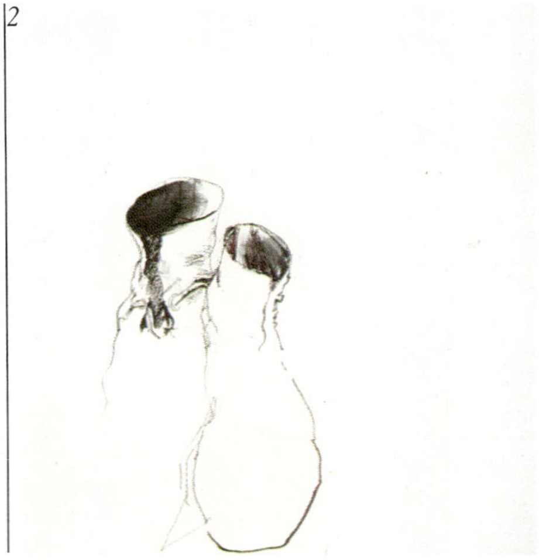

3

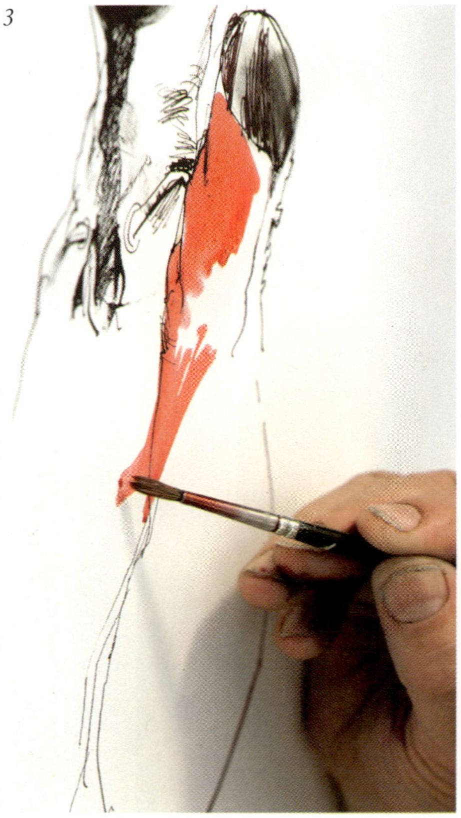

4

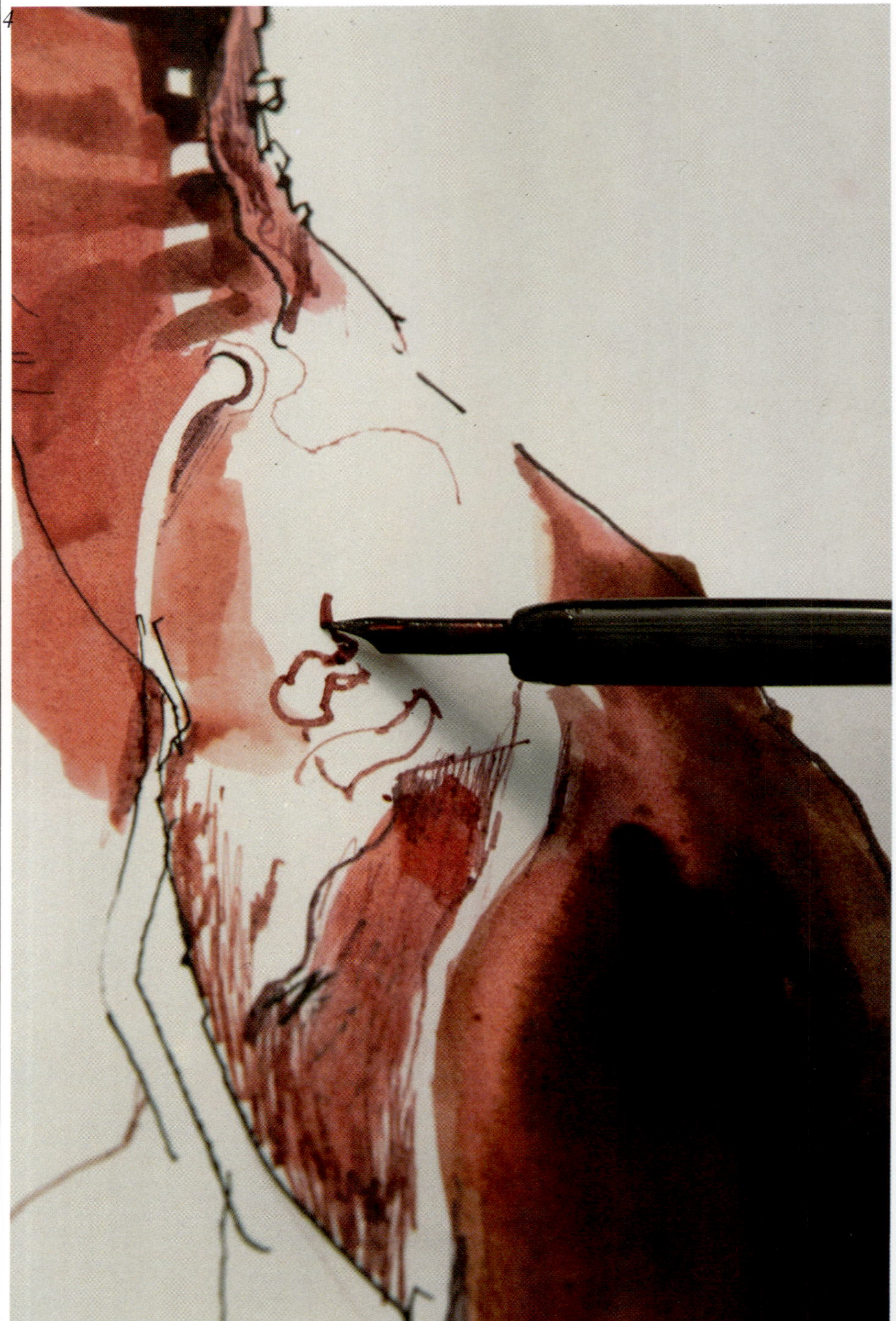

5

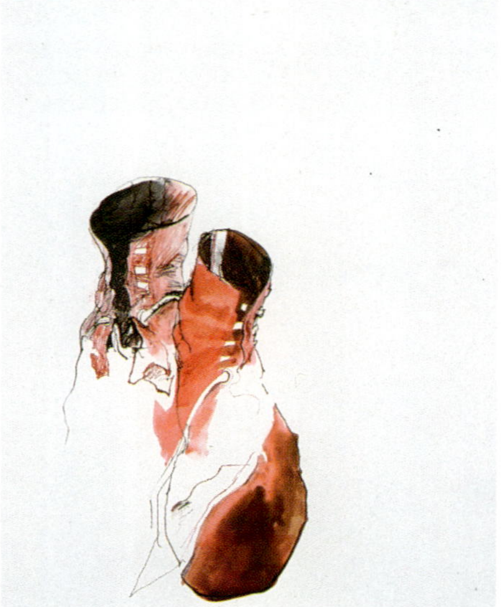

*Start the outline in black ink and a dip pen. Vary the line by moving the pen both quickly and slowly. Dip a brush in water and let the pen line bleed into the wetted area, to create the shadows (1). Continue with the outline, indicating the texture of the leather (2). Put in the preliminary wash with red ink (3). Using a pen, add linear details such as the laces (4). Mix a small amount of red and burnt sienna to develop the outline of the boot (5).*

6

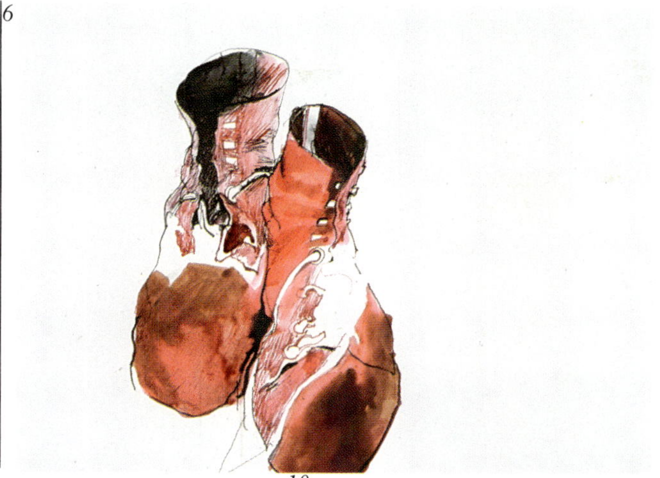

7

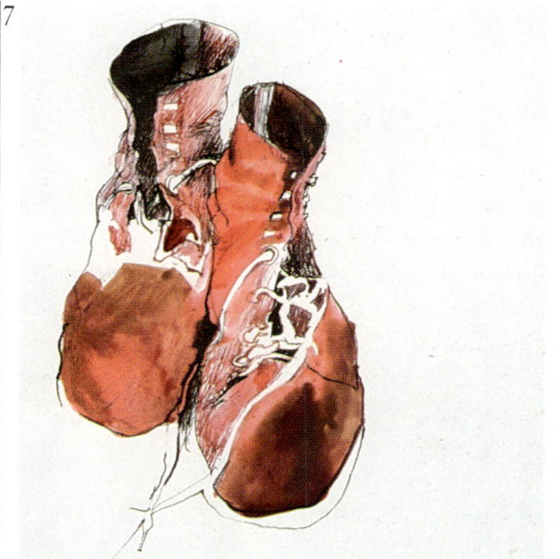

8

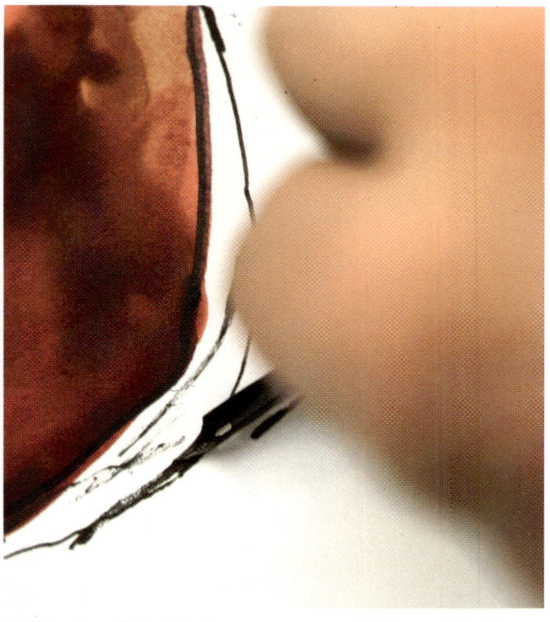

*With red and black ink, cross-hatch the remaining area of the right boot, leaving parts untouched to create laces and holes (6). Using the pen and black ink, work back into the shoe with cross-hatching strokes to create the area around the laces (7). By turning the nib on its back, you will be able to create a rough jagged line (8). Use this to describe the sole of the boots (9). Complete the picture by laying a darker wash over the shadow areas of the left boot (10).*

9

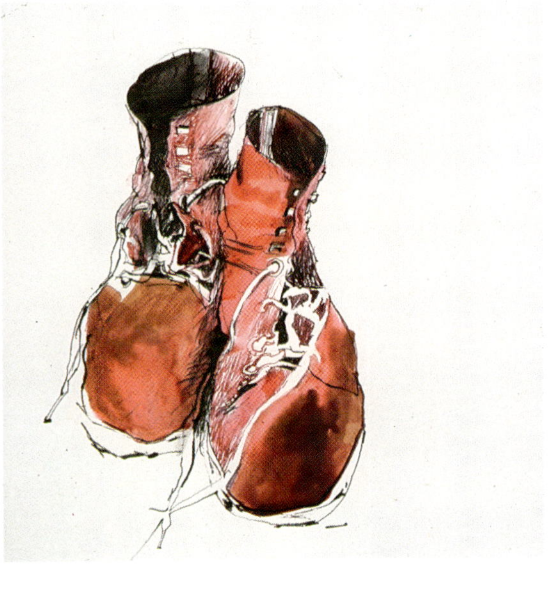

10

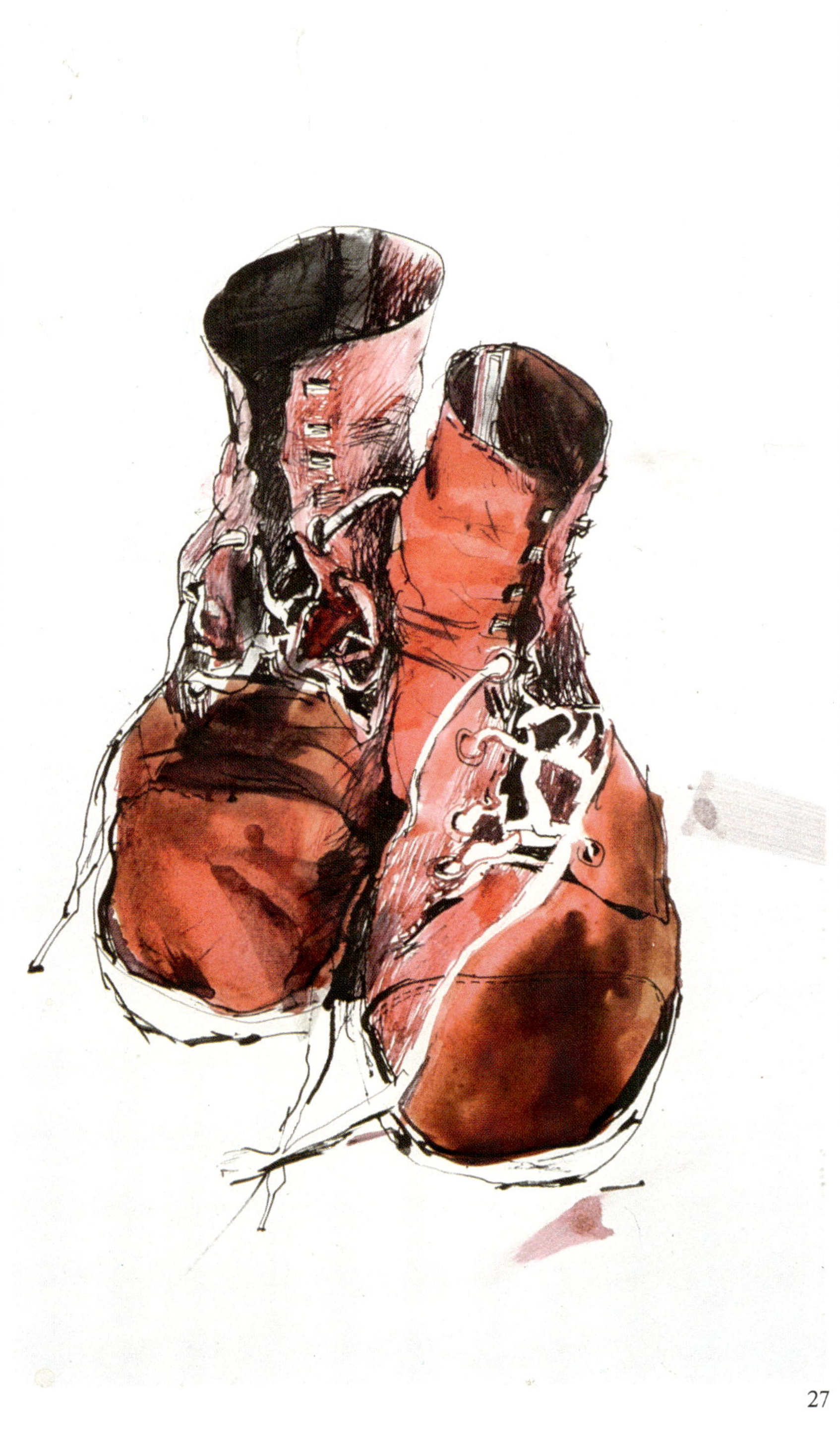

# STILL-LIFE IN WHITE

An all-white still-life presents an excellent opportunity for looking carefully at tone. Our artist chose a few simple objects — a plate, mug, bottles and a box — and gave them a coat of matt white emulsion beforehand. This eliminated any distracting reflections and ensured that the subject was of a uniform white tone.

The picture is executed in coloured pencils and, although line and the side of the pencil lead were used to develop tonal areas, the method of drawing is similar to the classic oil painting technique of laying down colours, one over another, to achieve new colours. This requires confidence, because once put down coloured pencils are difficult to erase.

A striking feature of the composition is the use of the white paper within the objects to describe the local colour and highlights. The result is a convincing composition in which the individual objects are securely located in space, and the character of the composition is accurately conveyed. An exercise such as this where observation and accuracy are called for is taxing, but it is an excellent way of sharpening your perception, noting and recording the fine gradations of tone around an object.

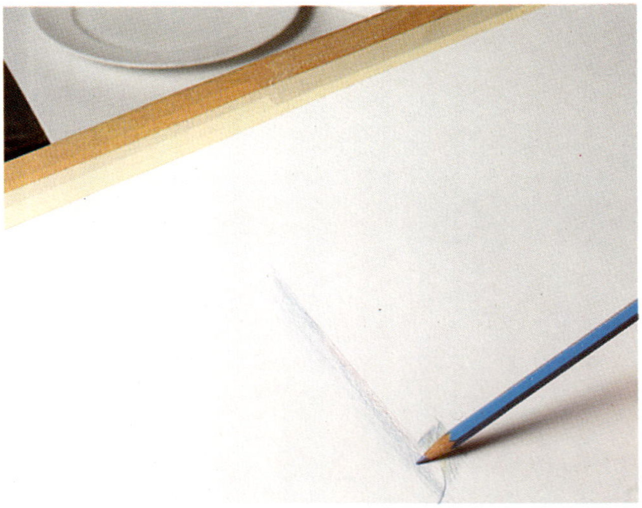

*Use a wide selection of coloured pencils for this exercise, giving yourself plenty of scope to make an exciting composition from the all-white subject. Use blue to sketch in the outlines* **(left)**, *keeping the objects large and central on the paper.*

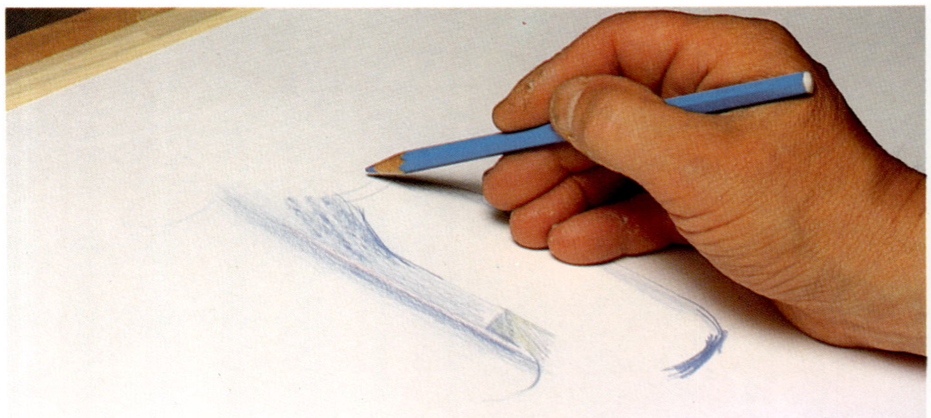

*Block in the background in the same colour* **(above)**. *This provides a solid tone to work into later with other colours.*

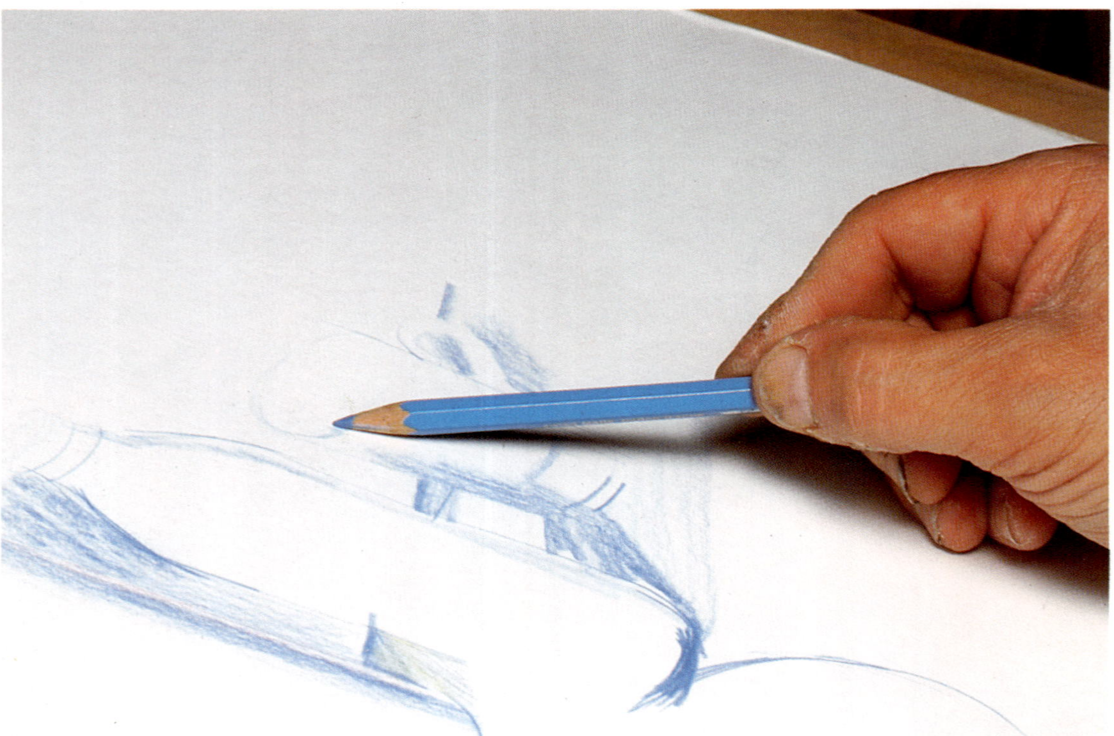

*Using the white paper as a light tone, draw into the outlines, laying in shadows to show the form of the objects* **(left)**.

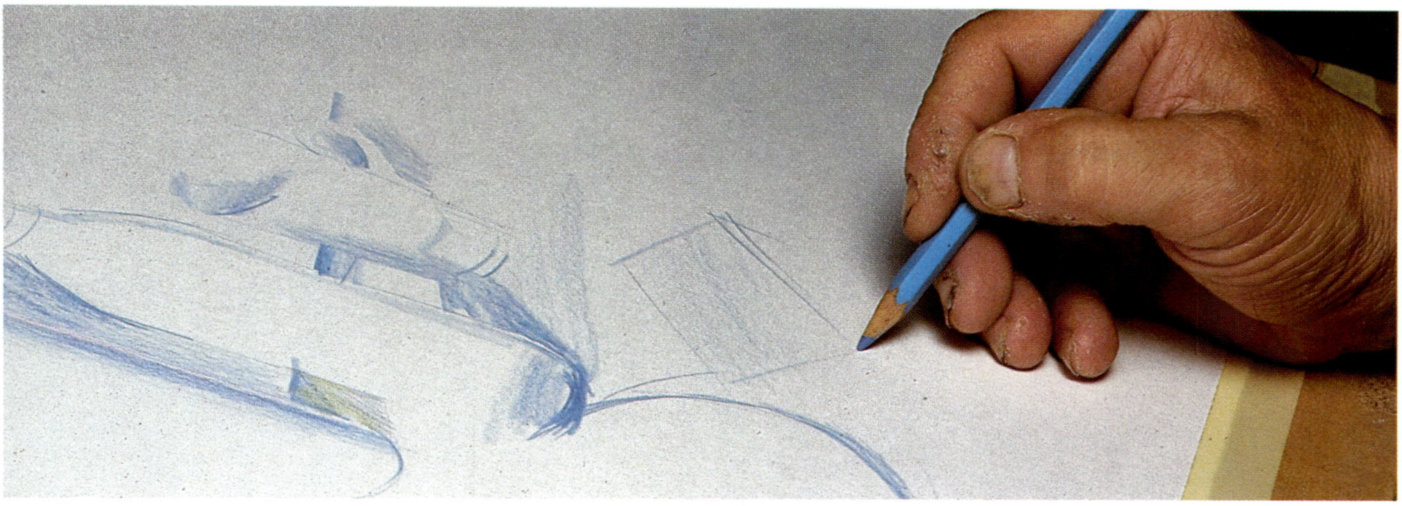

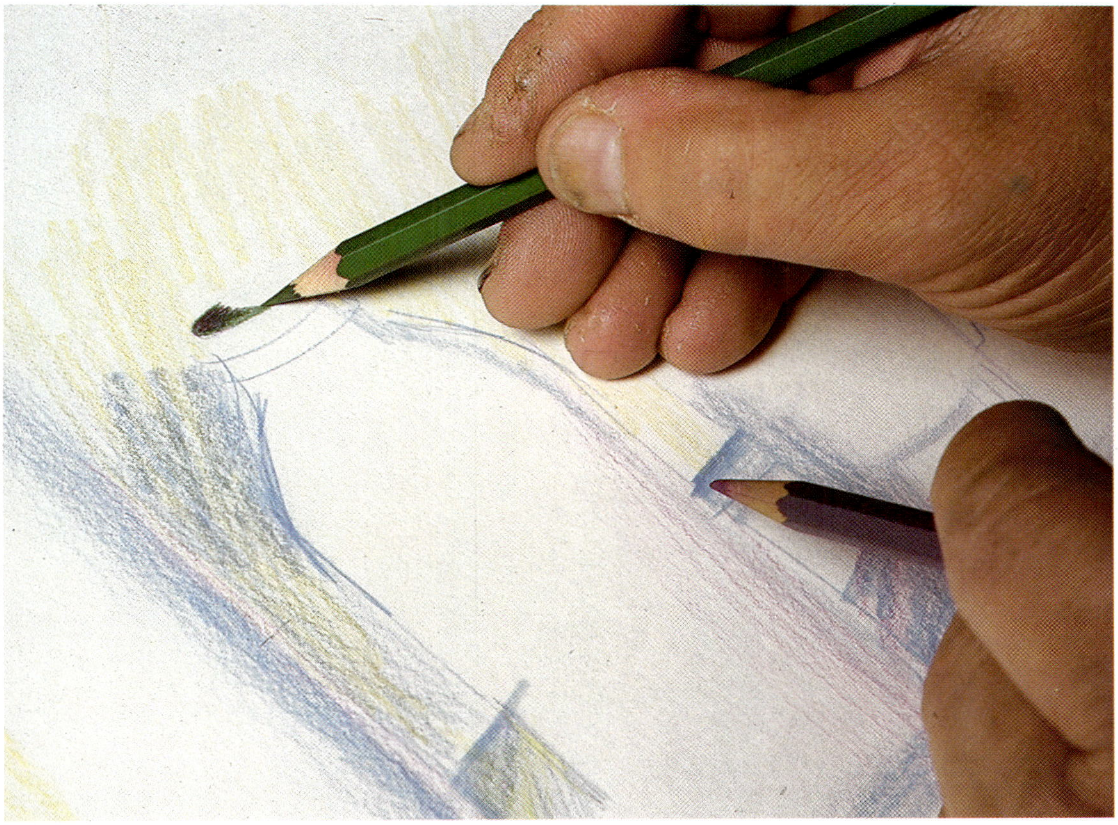

*Continue to define the drawing, making the lines and shadows quite hard and definite* **(above)**. *Look closely at the tones and reflections on the white objects. Try to differentiate between cool and warm areas, and to pick out any colours which may be reflected from the surrounding room. Close observation will often enable you to find subtle colour differences on the white surfaces. Introduce other colours into the drawing* **(left)**, *exaggerating the slight differences visible on the white.*

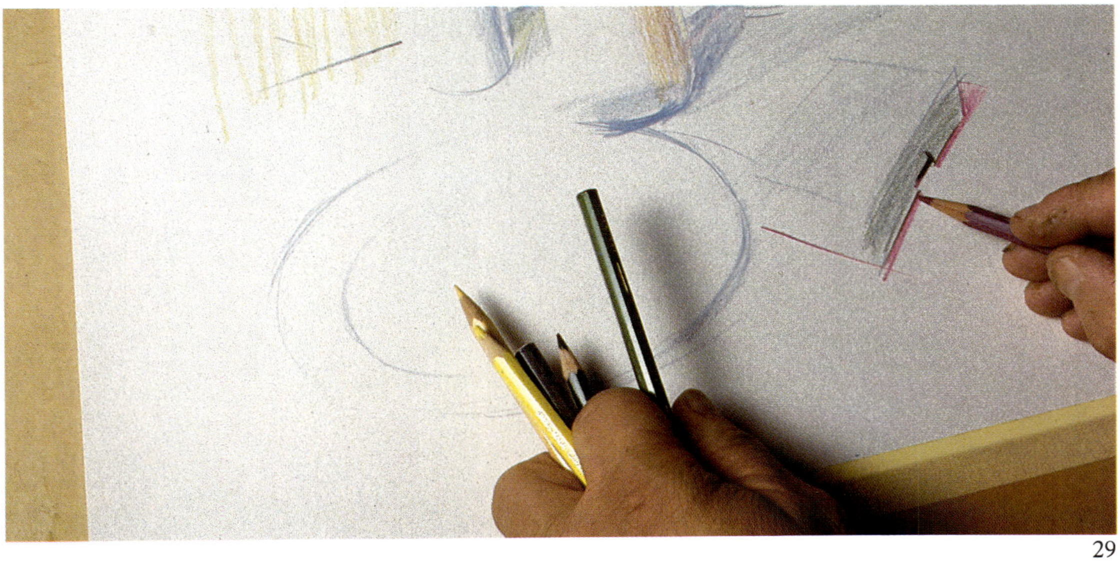

*Keeping broad differences between the cool and warm areas, use the coloured pencils to build up the shadows* **(right)**. *Many different colours can be used together without losing their separate identity or becoming muddy.*

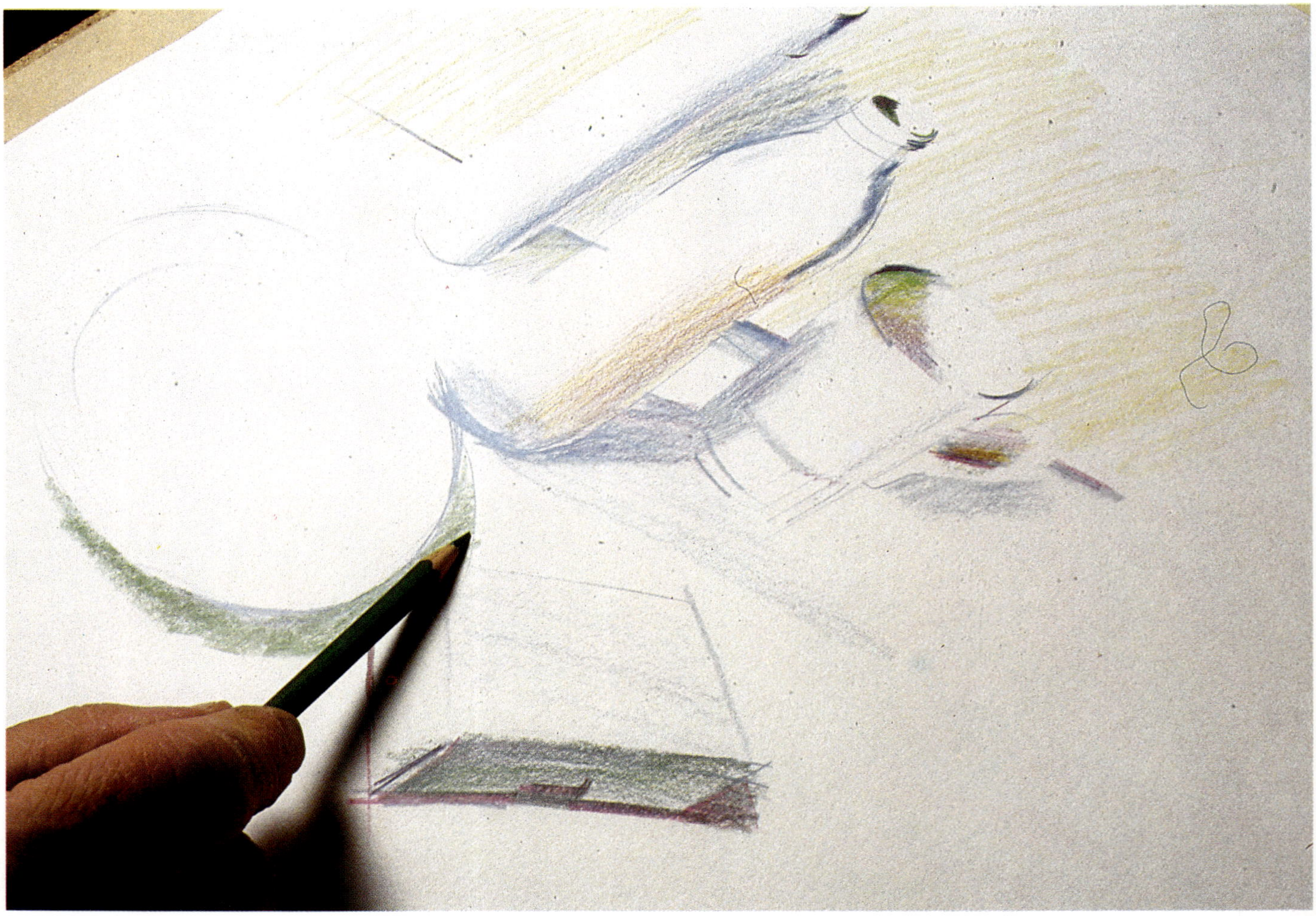

*Keep the pencils sharp to ensure crisp, distinct drawing. Use the darker colours to build up the sharp, clear edges of the objects* **(above)**. *Use coloured pencils to define the outline and obtain a finished effect* **(right)**. *Leave clear areas of white paper to maintain a crisp, clean quality.*

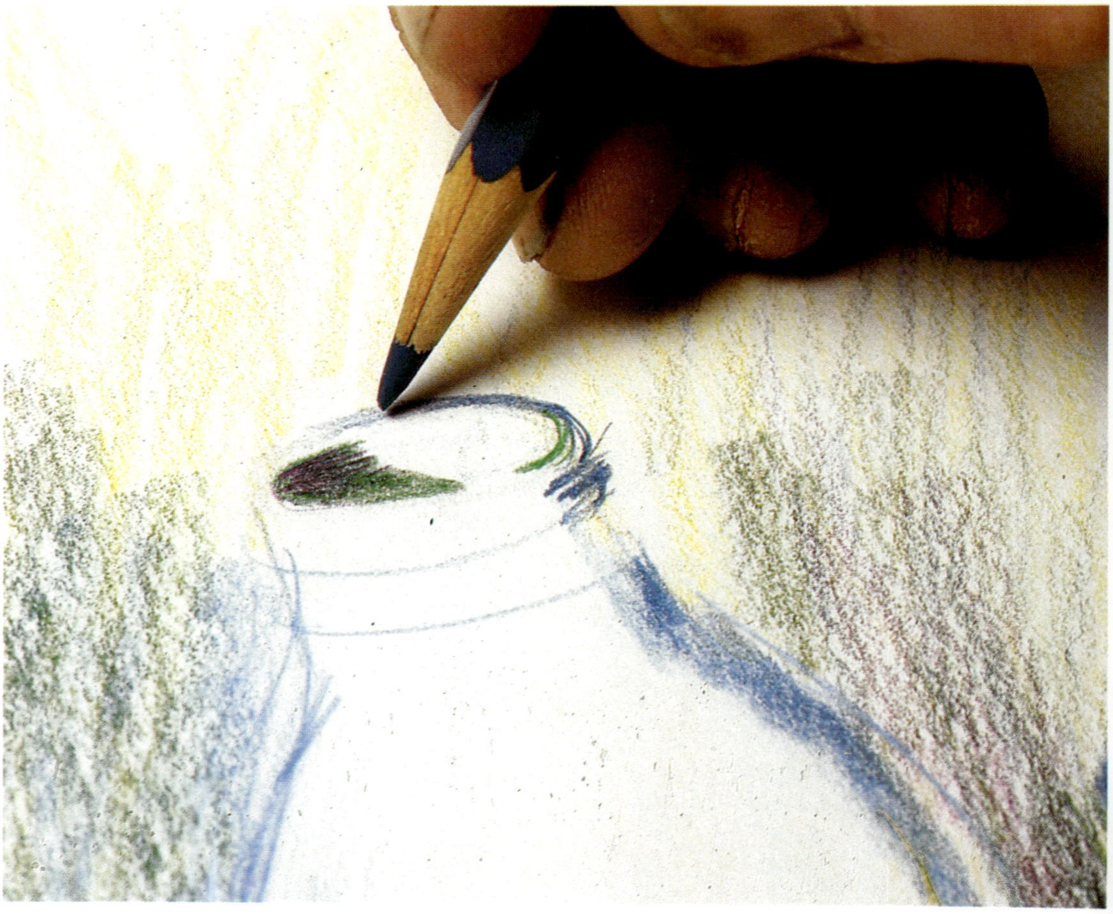

*Experiment with different colour combinations. Blues and purples used together produce cool shadows* **(right)***; reds and yellows combine to make vibrant, warm tones.*

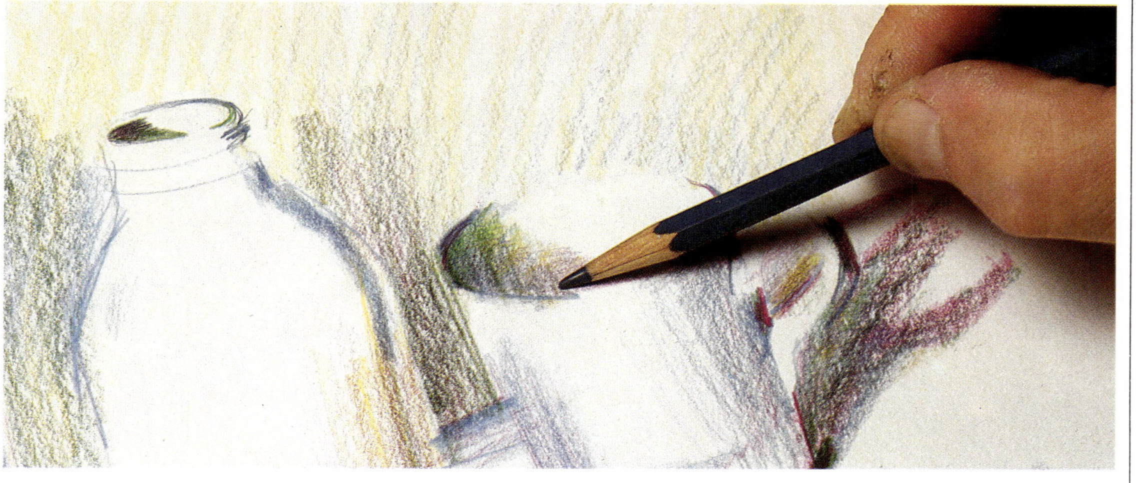

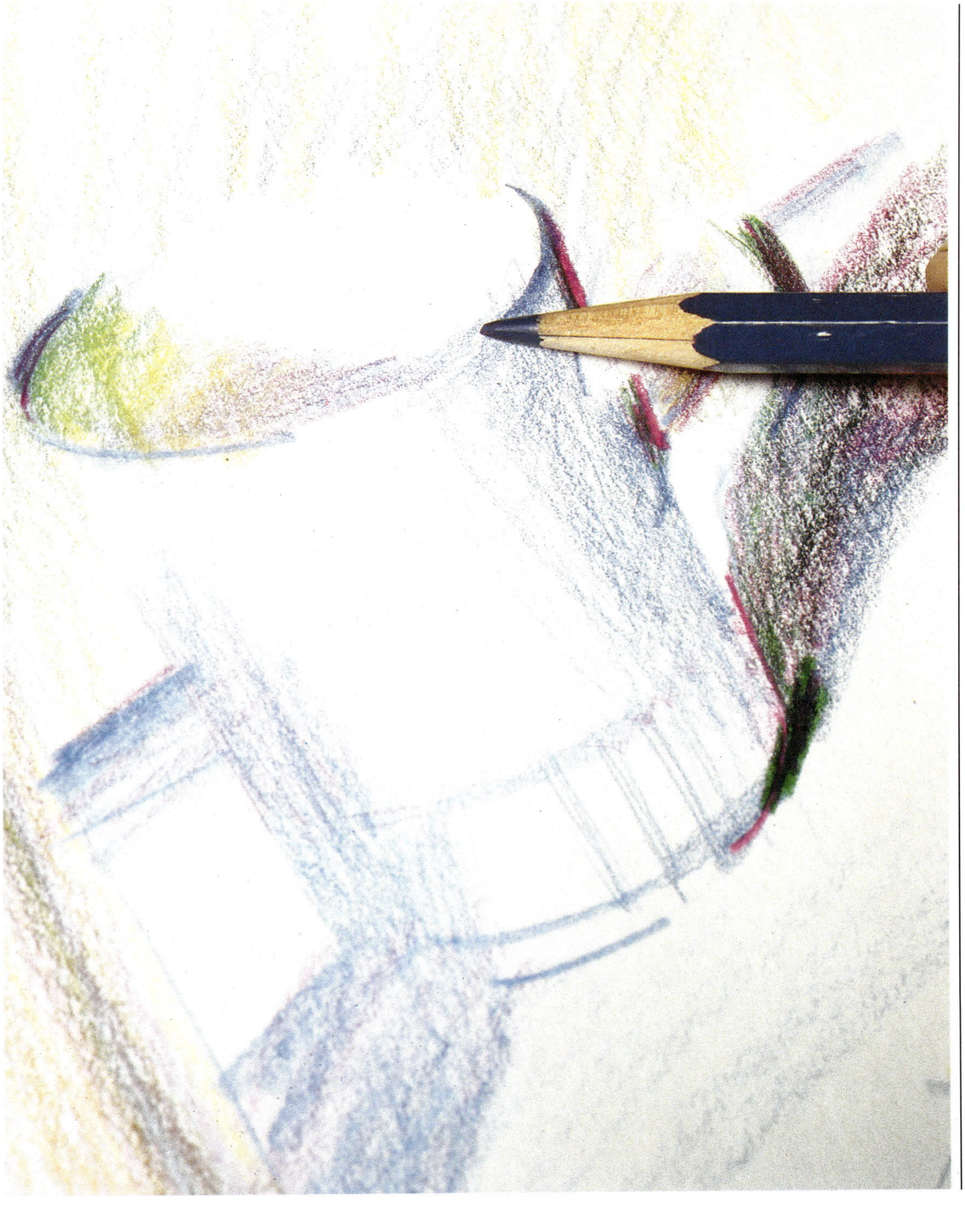

*It is important not to overwork your drawing. Too many layers of colour clog the surface of the paper and cannot be easily erased. Where the outline becomes lost, carefully redraw this with a sharpened pencil* **(left)**.

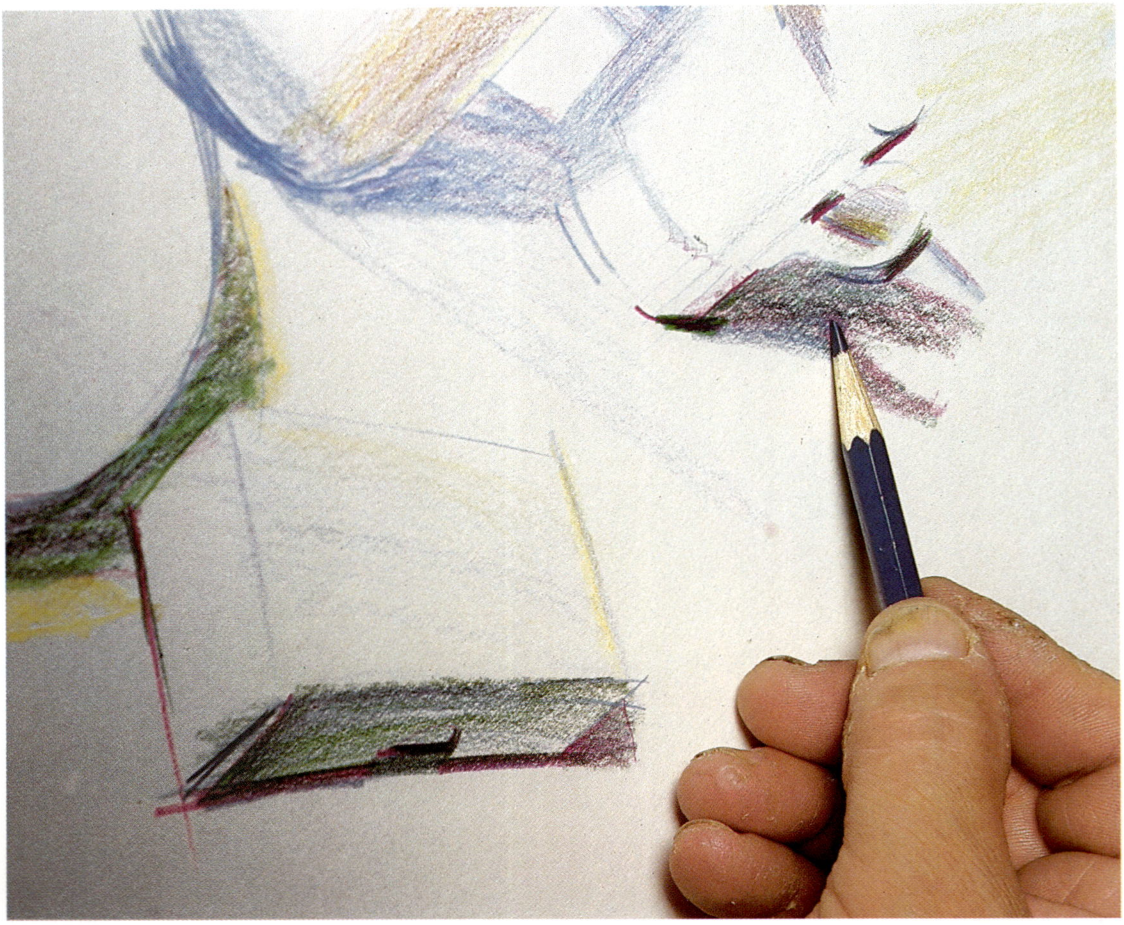

*Use complementary colours together to obtain a neutral effect. These neutral tones will not become muddy or dead if you allow the separate colours to show through and do not make the pencil strokes too dense* **(left)**.

*The finished drawing shows how colour can be used creatively when there is very little colour in the actual subject* **(below)**.

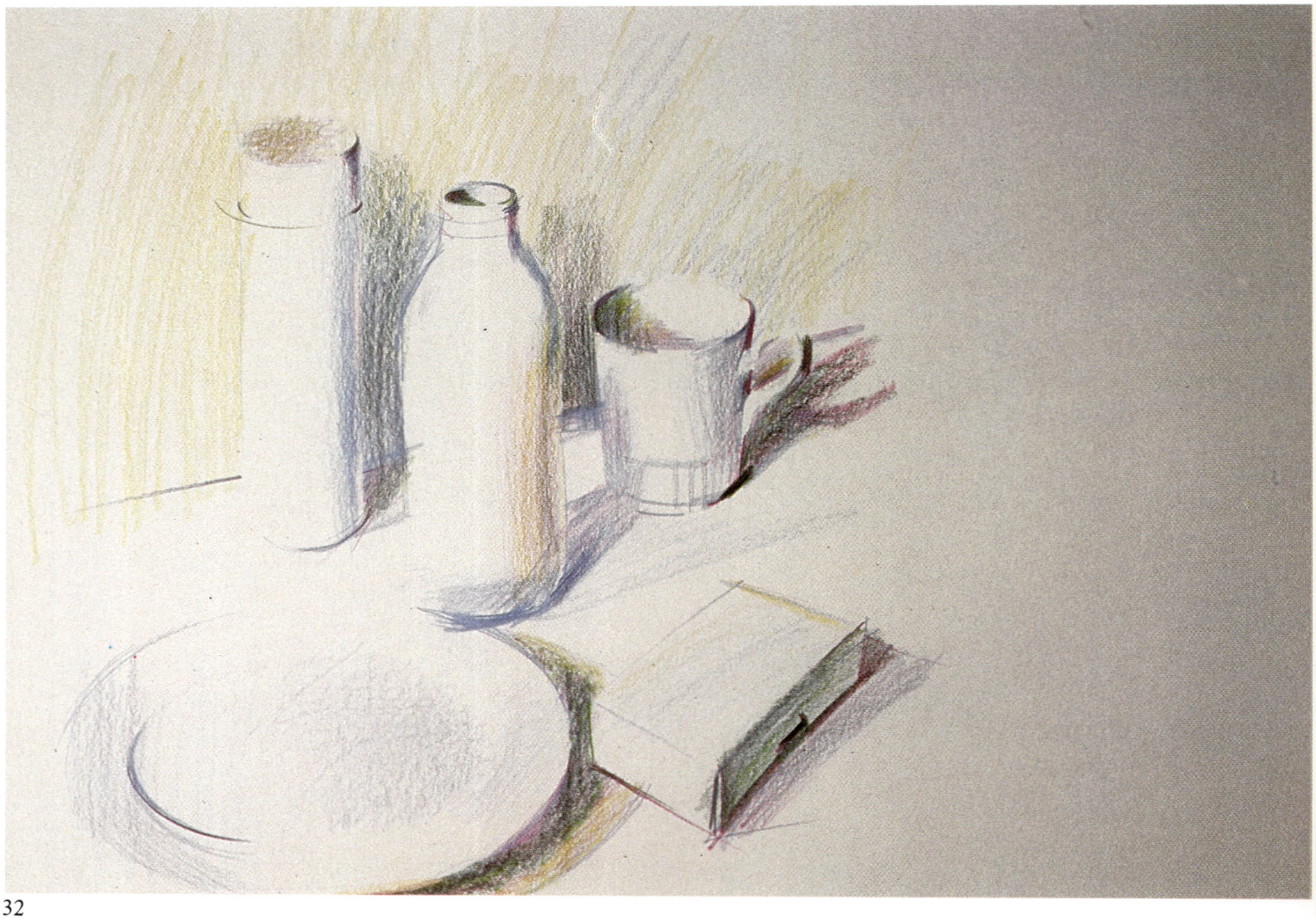